# Hangeul

## Korea's Unique Alphabet

KOREA ESSENTIALS No. 1

# **Hangeul:** Korea's Unique Alphabet

First Published in 2010 by Seoul Selection
B1 Korean Publishers Association Bldg., 105-2 Sagan-dong,
Jongno-gu, Seoul 110-190, Korea
Phone: (82-2) 734-9567
Fax: (82-2) 734-9562
Email: publisher@seoulselection.com
Website: www.seoulselection.com

ISBN: 978-89-91913-69-1    04080
ISBN: 978-89-91913-70-7    (set)
Printed in the Republic of Korea

# Hangeul

## Korea's Unique Alphabet

KOREA
FOUNDATION
한국국제교류재단

Seoul Selection

# CONTENTS

# INTRODUCTION

Writing is a cornerstone of civilization, a crucial invention that better allows peoples to accumulate and pass down knowledge and preserve cultures. It is a quintessentially human invention, but not a universal one: according to *Ethnologue: Languages of the World*, there are currently some 6,909 living languages in the world, yet only a minority of these are written, and of these just a handful have their own unique writing systems.

Hangeul, the indigenous writing system of Korea, is one of them. Promulgated in 1446, Hangeul is an ingenious system that utilizes forward-thinking and scientific linguistic theories and principles of Korean traditional culture to perfectly express the sounds of the Korean language. Invented by the brilliant King Sejong the Great, the alphabet has been widely lauded by scholars the world over for its advanced phonetic system and ease of use. Noted linguist Geoffrey Sampson, in his work *Writing Systems: A Linguistic Introduction*, went as far as to say, "Whether or not it is ultimately the best of all conceivable scripts for Korean, Hangeul must unquestionably rank as one of the great intellectual achievements of humankind."

This book will examine the unique characteristics of the Hangeul writing system and its impact on Korean society. We will first look at why many scholars regard Hangeul as the world's preeminent writing system. We will then examine the structure of the alphabet, exploring the linguistic and philosophical concepts that underlie it. We will survey the historical process by which Hangeul was invented and take an in-depth look at King Sejong the Great, the

Korean king widely credited with the creation of the writing system. After this, we will canvass the subsequent development of the alphabet over the ensuing centuries and study its impact on Korean culture and society. Lastly, we will observe how Hangeul has helped promote the use of information technology in Korea and look at the myriad ways in which the writing system inspires Korean culture and art, including genres like fashion and dance.

世·솅宗종御·엉製·졩訓·훈民민正·졍音흠

製·졩는 글지·슬 씨·니 御·엉製·졩는 님·금 지·스샨 그리·라 訓·훈은 フ르·칠·씨·오 民민운 百·빅姓·셩이·오 音흠은 소리·니 訓·훈民민正·졍音흠은 百·빅姓·셩 フ르·치시·논 正·졍훈 소리·라

國·귁之징語·엉音흠·이

國·귁은 나·라히·라 之징는 ·입·겨지·라 語·엉는 :말쓰미·라

나·랏:말쓰·미

異·잉乎흥中듕國·귁·ᄒ·야

異·잉는 다·ᄅᆞᆯ·씨·라 乎흥는 아·모그에 ·ᄒ·논 겨·체 ·ᄡᅳ·논 字·쫑ㅣ·라 中듕國·귁·

"Because the speech of this country is different from that of China, [the spoken language] doesn't match the [Chinese] letters. Therefore, even if the ignorant want to communicate, many of them in the end cannot state their concerns. Saddened by this, I have [had] 28 letters newly made. It is my wish that every man may easily learn these letters and that [they] be convenient for daily use."

From the *Hunminjeongeum* ("Proper Sounds for the Instruction of the People"), 1446

Chapter One

# KOREA'S UNIQUE WRITING SYSTEM

**W**erner Sasse, a German linguist and former professor at the Universität Hamburg, called the Korean writing system of Hangeul 한글 "the world's greatest writing system, devised on a foundation of traditional philosophical principles and scientific theories." Indeed, Sasse is just one of many scholars who have praised Korea's unique writing system. British linguist Geoffrey Sampson declared Hangeul to be a featural writing system and the most scientifically based of all writing systems. Dutch linguist Howard F. Vos also lauded Hangeul as the finest writing system in the world. Umeda Hiroyuki, of Japan's Reitaku University, has said that Hangeul is the most advanced phonemic writing system in the world and a featural writing system that is rated a step above the Roman script.

Why is so much praise heaped upon an alphabet created six centuries ago in a small East Asian kingdom? What are the characteristics of Hangeul that make it so special?

## RATIONAL STRUCTURE

Hangeul clearly differs from other writing systems in that the principles of both its creation and its intended usage were systematically established from the outset. As such, Hangeul features a highly rational structure that makes it easy for anyone in the world to learn and use. Most other alphabetic writing systems are the result of centuries of gradual evolution, and thus are not as systematically and rationally organized.

In Hangeul, the basic consonants take their shape from the configuration of the speech organs used for their articulation, while consonants expressing lenis, aspirated, and fortis sounds were created with intuitive and expressive shapes. These characteristics are truly extraordinary when viewed from the perspective of modern linguistic theory.

# ALPHABETS AROUND THE WORLD

The most widely used writing system today is the Roman script. Also called the Latin script, it is used in Western and Northern Europe, North and South America, Australia, various countries in Africa that were once the colonies of European powers, and other areas. Recently, Southeast Asian nations such as Vietnam, Indonesia, and Malaysia, as well as other countries like Turkey, have adopted the Roman script as a replacement for or supplement to their traditional writing system. The Roman script's growing worldwide usage is due in part to the fact that, as a phonetic writing system, it is relatively easy to learn and write; furthermore, the global expansion of Western culture over the past several centuries has also contributed much to its pervasive influence.

Other writing systems used by large numbers of people include Cyrillic, Indian, and Arabic script, as well as Chinese characters. Cyrillic script, like Roman script, is known to have originated from ancient Greek script, and is

ABC देवनागरी
ตัวอักษรไทย 한글 漢汉
αλφάβητο 字字
Кириллица ひ カ אלפבית
ら タ カ أبجدية
が カ
な ナ

used in nations of the former Soviet Union, including Russia. Other than Vietnam, Indonesia, and Malaysia, most Southeast Asian nations use an Indian script or a similar writing system. The writing systems used in these areas are presumed to have developed from the Indian Brahmi script. Middle Eastern countries such as Saudi Arabia have their own writing system, the Arabic script.

There might be various differences between nations and peoples, but their writing systems can often be traced back to a common source. In the East Asian region, Chinese characters have long been the standard writing system due to China's dominant influence. Japan has used both Chinese characters and its own writing systems, known collectively as Kana, which are derived from simplified Chinese characters.

- Latin
- Ethiopic
- Syllabaries
- Cyrillic
- North Indic
- Logographies
- Greek
- South Indic
- Arabic
- Hangeul

These characteristics make it easy for foreigners to learn to read and write Korean 한국어. Most people, when shown the relationship between letters of the Korean alphabet and the speech organs used to articulate them, as well as the method of combining letters into syllabic blocks, can quickly learn to read and write Hangeul (see p16).

# HANGEUL'S REMARKABLE CHARACTERISTICS

In the mid 1990s, the Linguistics, Philology & Phonetics Department of the University of Oxford, which is renowned for being at the forefront of linguistics research, evaluated 30 writing systems in terms of their rational, scientific, and unique characteristics. This study ranked Hangeul first.

Hangeul possesses several unique characteristics when compared with other writing systems.

### Purpose-Built

Perhaps the most notable characteristic of the Hangeul writing system, when compared to other writing systems around the world, is the systematic, scientific and historically documented process of its creation. Of 300 writing systems on the planet, most were not "created" per se; they developed over centuries, with little in the way of systematic planning. Hangeul represents an entirely new system; that is, it was created without imitating or adapting an existing writing system. In this regard, Hangeul is different, almost uniquely so. Records show it was created, if not by King Sejong the Great 세종대왕 himself, then by scholars commissioned by Sejong with the goal of promoting literacy amongst the royal subjects. It would be wrong to say that Hangeul is the only such "purpose-built" writing system—other nations, ethnic groups and even individuals have attempted to create their own writing systems. For instance, Yuan Emperor Kublai Khan commissioned Tibetan lama Drogön Chögyal Phagpa to create a unified script for his empire in 1269. Hangeul, however, is clearly the most successful and widely used of these endeavors, being used by 78 million Korean speakers in both South and North Korea as well as the Korean diaspora.

## Linguistically Scientific

As a writing system created with the express purpose of enabling the masses to read and teaching them the proper pronunciation of Korean words, the Hangeul system reflects a good deal of advanced knowledge of linguistics (see Chapter 2). It is a featural alphabet (see p18), which is to say that the shapes of its letters, far from being arbitrary, encode phonological features of the phonemes they represent. (For instance, the Korean consonants ㅋ and ㄲ are both based on ㄱ. ㅋ and ㄲ visually represent the attachment of phonetic features—aspiration and tenseness, respectively—through the addition of strokes.) It is, in fact, the only featural alphabet in wide use today.

Moreover, the process by which Hangeul was invented was noteworthy for its scientific basis and creativity. The shapes of the consonants are based on the shapes of the speech organs used for their articulation, while the vowels are related to the three symbols of heaven 하늘, earth 땅, and humanity 사람. According to the *Hunminjeongeum Haerye* ("Explanations and Examples of the Proper Sounds for the Instruction of the People"), promulgated in 1446 as an explanatory guide to the alphabet, the shapes of the consonants represent various speech organs, including the tongue, teeth and lips. Creating letters to represent the shapes of the speech organs used for their pronunciation was indeed a revolutionary innovation.

By way of contrast, the Latin alphabet—which originated on the Italian Peninsula in the seventh century BC and developed considerably

# How Hangeul's Letters are Formed

## I. Consonants

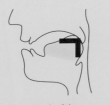

**Velar:** Back of the tongue pressed near the uvula.

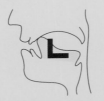

**Alveolar:** The tip of the tongue presses against the upper gums.

**Dental:** Sharp teeth.

**Bilabial:** Joined lips.

**Glottal:** Round-shaped throat.

\* The 17 consonants promulgated by King Sejong in 1444 have undergone phonological changes to become the 14 consonants of today's Hangeul.

| ㄱ | ㄴ | ㄷ | ㄹ | ㅁ | ㅂ | ㅅ |
|---|---|---|---|---|---|---|
| /g, k/ | /n/ | /d, t/ | /l, r/ | /m/ | /b, p/ | /s/ |

| ㅇ | ㅈ | ㅊ | ㅋ | ㅌ | ㅍ | ㅎ |
|---|---|---|---|---|---|---|
| /ng/ | /j/ | /ch/ | /k/ | /t/ | /p/ | /h/ |

## II. VOWELS

Heaven 天
Earth 地
Humanity 人

The three basic vowel characters of •, —, and | were created to symbolize the trinity of heaven, earth, and humanity, while philosophical principles were applied to create the remainder of the vowels.

| | + • = ᅡ [ㅏ] | | + •| = ᅣ [ㅑ] |
|---|---|

| + • = ㅏ [ㅏ]          | + |• = ㅑ [ㅑ]

• + | = ㅓ [ㅓ]          | + •| = ㅕ [ㅕ]

• + — = ㅗ [ㅗ]          | + ㅗ = ㅛ [ㅛ]

— + • = ㅜ [ㅜ]          | + ㅜ = ㅠ [ㅠ]

| ㅏ | ㅑ | ㅓ | ㅕ | ㅗ | ㅛ | ㅜ | ㅠ | — | | |
|---|---|---|---|---|---|---|---|---|---|
| /a/ | /ya/ | /eo/ | /yeo/ | /o/ | /yo/ | /u/ | /yu/ | /eu/ | /i/ |

in the following centuries—was a development upon the Etruscan alphabet, which itself was based on the Greek alphabet, which in turn was developed from the Phoenician alphabet, where the consonant characters were based on Egyptian hieroglyphs. Little or no planning went into the Latin alphabet's development, and individual letters give few clues as to their pronunciation. (Indeed, different languages pronounce individual letters in a different ways.)

As a featural alphabet, Hangeul bears some similarities with scientifically created writing systems invented centuries later, such as the Visible Speech system invented by Alexander Melville Bell (the father of telephone inventor Alexander Graham Bell) to teach the hearing impaired to speak.

### Easy to Learn

Unlike Chinese characters, which are logograms (essentially pictures), and the Japanese syllabaries of Katakana and Hiragana,

## WHAT IS A FEATURAL WRITING SYSTEM?

A "featural writing system" is one in which the symbols that compose the system represent not phonemes—the segmental units of sound that make up utterances—but rather "features," or the components of phonemes, which are considered by some linguists to be the smallest components of speech. Features include things such as voicing, aspiration and articulation. In the case of Hangeul, letters are composed of symbols that represent articulatory features—indeed, the letters are said to represent the position of organs of speech—which are in turn combined to form syllable blocks.

Featural alphabets are rare; most are relatively recent inventions created for use as shorthand or, in the case of Visible Speech, to teach the hearing impaired to speak. The Hangeul writing system is, in fact, the only featural writing system in common use today.

the Hangeul writing system is a full-fledged phonemic alphabet. Hangeul is a phonemic writing system with a unique structure that visually expresses syllables by transcribing the initial, medial, and final sounds together as a single unit (see p27). Thus, it has the advantages of a phonemic writing system as well as a syllabic system. The shapes of the letters are highly systematic, while the sounds that are related to one another share similarities. Hangeul is based on a dual structure of basic letters from which the remaining letters are derived (see p16).

In addition, Hangeul features a unique operating method that joins letters together by syllable to create yet another character; this is referred to as "joined writing." Hangeul consists of phonetic letters that are divided into consonants and vowels and joined together to form syllabic blocks. As such, this method of writing allows for easy reading and quick learning.

It is also remarkably easy to learn—as the *Hunminjeongeum Haerye* puts it, "A wise man can acquaint himself with them before

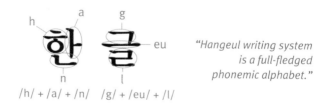

h — 한 — a    g — 글 — eu
        n            l

/h/ + /a/ + /n/   /g/ + /eu/ + /l/

*"Hangeul writing system is a full-fledged phonemic alphabet."*

**Chinese Character**

漢 字

/han/   /zi/

**Japanese Writing System**

ひらがな

/hi/  /ra/  /ga/  /na/

the morning is over; a stupid man can learn them in the space of ten days." While learning the Korean language itself requires considerably more study, learning to pronounce Korean words— any Korean word, in fact—requires just a few days of study. This is in large part thanks to Hangeul's orderly, rational system: pronunciation rules are regular, and unlike Western languages, there are very few exceptions that must be learned.

Hangeul's excellence is based on the fact that it is both easy to learn and easy to use, resulting in an illiteracy rate of essentially zero in Korea, and also includes the advantages of a phonetic writing system, which enables it to express practically any other language. For example, Japanese consists of about 350 syllables and Chinese includes some 420 syllables, nearly all of which can be expressed perfectly in Hangeul. For these reasons it is a marvelous writing system that has gained attention the world over.

It is also quick and easy to input Hangeul characters using a computer keyboard or cell phone keypad, and Hangeul is well suited for voice-recognition software that is used to convert verbal speech into writing (see Chapter 6).

# What Scholars Say About Hangeul

*"Whether or not it is ultimately the best of all conceivable scripts for Korean, Hangeul must unquestionably rank as one of the great intellectual achievements of humankind."*

Geoffrey Sampson, linguist/professor, University of Sussex

*"Hangeul is the world's greatest writing system, devised on a foundation of traditional philosophical principles and scientific theories."*

Werner Sasse, former professor, University of Hamburg

*"Hangeul is the most advanced phonemic writing system in the world, and a featural writing system that is rated a step above Roman writing."*

Umeda Hiroyuki, President, Reitaku University

*"Koreans invented the solely creative and amazing alphabetic writing system called Hangeul for the Korean people. Hangeul is perhaps the most scientific system of writing in general use in any country."*

Edwin O. Reischauer, historian/professor, Harvard University

*"Hangeul is the best alphabet that all the languages have dreamed of."*

John Man, historian/author of *Alpha Beta: How 26 Letters Shaped the Western World*

*"This is the simplest and best set of characters in the world."*

Pearl Buck, author of *The Good Earth*

# 2

Chapter Two

# STRUCTURE OF THE HANGEUL SYSTEM

Hangeul consists of 14 consonants and 10 vowels, but if we break these letters down we find that they are based on the five basic consonants 자음 of ㄱ[k, g], ㄴ[n], ㅁ[m], ㅅ[s], and ㅇ[ŋ] and the three basic vowels 모음 of ·[ɐ], ㅡ[i], and ㅣ[i], with extra letters formed according to their phonetic features.

## Consonants

Hangeul is based on five basic consonants, each of which takes its shape from the speech organ used to articulate its sound, while additional consonants can be created by doubling the consonant symbols and/or adding strokes.

For example, a line indicating aspiration is added to ㄱ to produce ㅋ, and by doubling the ㄱ it is possible to produce its tense counterpart ㄲ. In this way, the phonetic similarity between the sounds represented by ㄱ and ㅋ is highlighted, making Hangeul one of the easiest writing systems to learn.

Consonants were based on the shape of the speech organ used for their vocalization or the change in the shape of the organ as the sound was vocalized. The consonants were divided into four categories for each of the five basic consonants of ㄱ (velar sound), ㄴ (alveolar sound), ㅁ (labial sound), ㅅ (dental sound), and ㅇ (glottal sound), as well as the characteristics of their sounds. These four categories, which do not correspond exactly to English phonetic category terms, included weak plosives, strong plosives, voiced consonants, and a category that includes nasal and liquid sounds. The combination of the basic consonants and additional strokes allow for the creation of dozens more consonants.

## Vowels

The three basic vowels ( · , ─, and ㅣ ) take their shape from heaven, earth and humanity. These three basic letters were used to form other vowels based on philosophical principles related to the complementarity of *yin* and *yang*, the five elements (metal 쇠, water 물, wood 나무, fire 불, and earth 흙), and the five directions (east 동, west 서, south 남, north 북, and center 중앙).

The basic vowels are combined to create further vowel symbols. For this reason, Hangeul became known in the late 20th century as a "featural writing system," one step above other phonemic (alphabetic) writing systems. The method of analyzing the ontological unit of phonemes according to the abstract and discriminatory unit of features was only recognized with the advent of the 20th century. Sejong's originality in establishing this method theoretically and using it to invent a writing system in the 15th century thus deserves to be called the victory of a scientific spirit that transcended its era.

# HANGEUL'S DESIGN

## I. CONSONANTS

$ㄴ + \bullet → \dot{ㄴ} = ㄷ$

$ㅅ + \bullet → \dot{ㅅ} = ㅈ$

$ㄱ + \bullet → \dot{ㄱ} = ㅋ$

$ㄷ + \bullet → \dot{ㄷ} = ㅌ$

$ㅈ + \bullet → \dot{ㅈ} = ㅊ$

$ㄱ + ㄱ = ㄲ$

$ㄷ + ㄷ = ㄸ$

$ㅂ + ㅂ = ㅃ$

* As a featural writing system, Hangeul's structure is systematized so that new letters are created by adding discriminatory features to existing letters, which enables it to most effectively express all of the sounds needed for the Korean language.

## II. Vowels

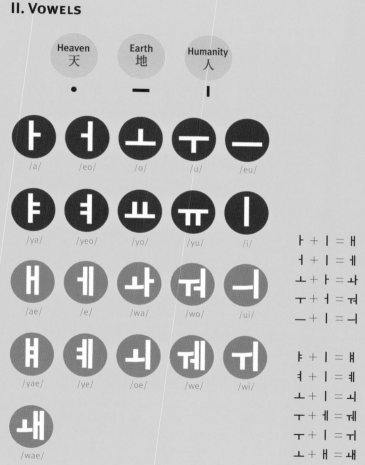

| Heaven 天 | Earth 地 | Humanity 人 |
| :---: | :---: | :---: |
| • | — | ǀ |

/a/  /eo/  /o/  /u/  /eu/

/ya/  /yeo/  /yo/  /yu/  /i/

/ae/  /e/  /wa/  /wo/  /ui/

/yae/  /ye/  /oe/  /we/  /wi/

/wae/

ㅏ + ㅣ = ㅐ
ㅓ + ㅣ = ㅔ
ㅗ + ㅏ = ㅘ
ㅜ + ㅓ = ㅝ
ㅡ + ㅣ = ㅢ

ㅑ + ㅣ = ㅒ
ㅕ + ㅣ = ㅖ
ㅗ + ㅣ = ㅚ
ㅜ + ㅔ = ㅞ
ㅜ + ㅣ = ㅟ
ㅗ + ㅐ = ㅙ

## Combination

Hangeul is an alphabet, but it employs a writing system slightly different from that employed by other alphabets. In most alphabets, the consonants and vowels are written separately to express a variety of sounds. In the case of Latin, Egyptian, Greek and other typical alphabets, consonants and vowels are written out in a line.

Hangeul isn't written like this, however. In Hangeul, consonants and vowels are grouped together into clusters. Hangeul can be written either horizontally or vertically, while the combination of these vowels and consonants and the space that each letter occupies in each syllabic block are highly systematic. Syllables can be made up of an initial consonant, a medial vowel, and a final consonant; the initial consonant (either a consonant or a silent placeholder for a vowel) and medial vowel are mandatory, while a final consonant is optional.

So Hangeul is written as follows, with the starting sound, middle sound and ending sound of each syllable written as a cluster:

With this manner of writing, Hangeul was able to take on the function of syllabic writing and, likewise, could be used easily to express Chinese words.

## Versatile Writing System

Hangeul is a user-friendly writing system that allows the expression not only of the vocal sounds of people, but of natural sounds as well, like a bird singing or the sound of wind. Hangeul is also flexible enough to be expanded to express sounds that may not exist in Korean but do exist in other languages, such as Chinese. Thus, Hangeul can use its eight basic letters to create the 11,172 distinct syllables in common use according to the Unicode 2.0 standard. (Unicode is a standard international writing system that allows computers to consistently express all of the world's languages.) This is possible because Hangeul uses a system that combines a few basic phonemes to form syllabic blocks.

At first glance it may look simple, but in order to devise this system from scratch, Sejong needed not only an abundant knowledge of phonetics but also a revolutionary "digital mindset," which recognized individual sounds as complexes of abstract features.

## PLACEMENT

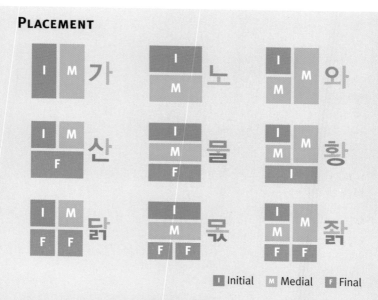

I Initial    M Medial    F Final

* Consonants and vowels are written together in syllabic units, which enable horizontal, vertical, and complex combinations. It is also possible to write one individual character after another and have the result still be legible.

# 3

## Chapter Three

# INVENTION OF HANGEUL

The writing systems used in most civilized societies today are alphabets that have been developed by many people over a long period of time from ancient writing systems, such as Sumerian and Egyptian. It is only natural that many nations and peoples would choose alphabetic writing systems, since they are the crystallization of millennia of human wisdom. By contrast, Hangeul was created in 1443 in the small East Asian nation of Korea as the product of the scientific research of one man, King Sejong the Great.

Hangeul is not the result of following in the footsteps of past writing systems but the product of a revolution in the leading linguistic theory of the time in East Asia: the theory of Chinese phonetics. In this regard, the invention of Hangeul can be seen as an epochal event in the linguistic history of the world. Yet even more amazing is the modern, rational spirit that its inventor, King Sejong, possessed.

# WHAT WAS THERE BEFORE HANGEUL?

Prior to the creation of the Hangeul writing system—and, indeed, even after it—the primary medium of formal correspondence in Korea was classical Chinese, which was based on Chinese as it was used in the Zhou (1045-256 BC) and Han (206 BC-AD 220) Dynasties. In East Asia, classical Chinese played a similar role to that of Latin in medieval Europe: it was the language of learning, law, and international communication, even in nations—like Korea—that did not speak Chinese, or even a related language. The impact classical Chinese had on Korean culture, both ancient and contemporary, was profound: even after the creation of the revolutionary Hangeul alphabet, classical Chinese continued to serve as Korea's literary and administrative language until just before the turn of the 20th century. In deeply Confucian Korea, knowledge of classical Chinese was required for understanding the Confucian classics, a sine qua non for political office and social influence.

Classical Chinese required a good deal of study to master—the kind of time only the very wealthy could afford—which resulted in

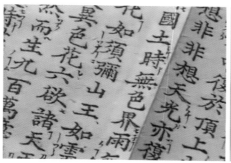

Left: The obsolete Idu writing sytem, seen as small annotations to the side of the Chinese characters
Right: Silla scholar Seol Chong, who is credited with its systemization

literacy being confined to just a small elite of Korean society. To write the Korean language, meanwhile, a system known as Idu 이두 was used. Idu was systematized by the scholar Seol Chong during the reign of King Sinmun (r. 681-691) of the Silla Kingdom. It used Chinese characters, with some special characters, to represent Korean phonology. While the writing system was in common use from the Silla period to the creation of Hangeul in the Joseon era, especially amongst the middle class, it was unwieldy and difficult—some Chinese characters were used based on their Chinese sound, others based on their meaning, and some were even given new sounds and meanings. Chinese characters also proved unsuited to representing Korean grammar. With the adoption of the much superior Hangeul writing system, Idu fell out of use.

## INVENTION OF HANGEUL

The writing system that Koreans today know as Hangeul was previously referred to as Hunminjeongeum 훈민정음. Hunminjeongeum is the only writing system in the world for which the name of its creator and the date of its invention are specifically known, earning it an unparalleled distinction among world writing systems.

In 1443, King Sejong, the fourth monarch of the Joseon Dynasty (1392-1910), unveiled Hunminjeongeum. This fact is recorded in the section on the ninth month of the 28th year of the reign of Sejong, in Book 113 of the *Sejongsillok* 세종실록 ("The Annals of King Sejong"), a 163-volume chronicle of Sejong's reign compiled by some 60 court officials. This is also set forth in the following passage at the end of the *Hunminjeongeum Haerye* ("Explanations and Examples of the Proper Sounds for the Instruction of the People"), a book written by Jeong In-ji (1396-1478), a Joseon

Dynasty civil official and scholar, which explains the purpose for creating the writing system and describes its usage: "In the winter of the year 1443, our king invented 28 characters of proper sounds...and called them Hunminjeongeum."

After inventing the alphabet and writing system, Sejong instructed the scholars of the Jiphyeonjeon 집현전 ("The Hall of Worthies"— see p34), a research institute of the royal court, to prepare an instructional guide for the new writing system. This guide was *Hunminjeongeum*, which was published in the ninth lunar month of the year 1446. In Book 102 of the *Sejongsillok*, in the section on the twelfth month of the 25th year of the king's reign, it is recorded, "In this month, the king himself created an alphabet of twenty-eight symbols... He calls it Hunminjeongeum." These records suggest that Sejong himself invented the writing system and named it Hunminjeongeum.

*Hunminjeongeum Haerye*

# WHO ACTUALLY CREATED THE ALPHABET?

While we believe that Sejong commissioned the Jiphyeonjeon to formulate the Hangeul writing system, and that the project was completed in late 1443 or early 1444, the role King Sejong personally played in the development of the writing system is subject to debate. When asked who invented the Hangeul writing system, most Koreans will answer, "King Sejong." When asked to choose between King Sejong and the scholars of the Jiphyeonjeon, however, most do not know how to answer. Within academia, too, there is disagreement as to who, exactly, did what.

The reason for the disagreement is that there are no detailed records explaining the process through which the writing system was formulated. The *Hunminjeongeum Haerye*, in fact, doesn't appear until three years after the alphabet was created.

### Theory 1

One theory has it that King Sejong created the Hangeul alphabet by himself. This theory is supported by the *The Annals of the Joseon Dynasty* 조선왕조실록, the official history of the Joseon era, which states that King Sejong personally created the 28-letter alphabet. A variation on this theory is that Sejong himself created the actual characters, while the scholars of the Jiphyeonjeon formulated how they would be used. Both theories have been criticized, however—it is difficult to believe a king could carry out such a

King Sejong the Great

project all by himself, and, likewise, the creation of an alphabet and the formulation of its use are intimately linked, which is an argument against Sejong having crafted the alphabet but allowed the Jiphyeonjeon to figure out how to use it.

## Theory 2

Another theory has it that the scholars of the Jiphyeonjeon crafted the Hangeul alphabet but "dedicated" it to Sejong, who was known to be ill at the time with what today appears to be diabetes. This is not impossible, especially when one considers the almost total prestige enjoyed by the kings of Joseon. That said, it is clear— based on his refutation of a scholar's argument against the new writing system (see p54)— that Sejong was a competent linguistic scholar, and the theory that Sejong was

In a period painting, scholars of the Jiphyeonjeon enjoy a brief respite from the rigors of academic pursuit.

personally uninvolved raises the question of why *The Annals of the Joseon Dynasty* would so clearly state that Sejong "personally" created the alphabet.

## Theory 3

Yet another theory has it that the creation of the Hangeul writing system was a project pursued in secret by the royal family—namely, Sejong, his three sons, and his daughter. According to this theory, the Jiphyeonjeon handled only the standardization of Chinese

## THE HALL OF WORTHIES, KING SEJONG'S BRILLIANT THINK TANK

The scholars of the Jiphyeonjeon give detailed explanations and examples of the new alphabet, Hangeul.

The Jiphyeonjeon, or Hall of Worthies, is usually credited with playing a major role in the creation of the Hangeul writing system. But what was this body of scholars, exactly?

The Jiphyeonjeon's history goes back to the late Goryeo era (918-1392), but it really came into its own under King Sejong, who expanded the institution in 1420 and turned it into a real research body. The actual number of officials who served at the Jiphyeonjeon fluctuated for a time, but it was set at 20 in 1436.

The Jiphyeonjeon was, first and foremost, an institute dedicated to cultivating scholars and producing academic research. Its most important duties were *gyeongyeon* and *seoyeon*. *Gyeongyeon* meant providing a place for the king and his retainers to discuss the Confucian classics so that the king might build up his Confucian education and, it was hoped, engage in proper politics. *Seoyeon*, meanwhile, was the education of the Crown Prince, who would eventually become king. The scholars of the Jiphyeonjeon also prepared diplomatic documents and served as examiners for the all-important *gwageo* civil service exam. As the Jiphyeonjeon was located in the palace and the scholars were noted for their writing, some of them served as royal secretaries. It also took the lead in academic projects, such as researching into the political systems of ancient China and compiling books.

For the convenience of the scholars, Sejong purchased or printed a good many books and stored them at the Jiphyeonjeon. To young, talented officials, he granted the benefit of *saga dokseo*—time off from their official duties so that they might study, often at quiet temples in the mountains. In this manner, many talented scholars were produced by the Jiphyeonjeon.

After Sejong had been on the throne for 20 years, the Jiphyeonjeon began to take on a political role as well. In 1442, Sejong—his health beginning to fail—established a body, headed by the crown prince, to which he could delegate administrative duties. The scholars of the Jiphyeonjeon were able to use this body, on which they served, to wield political influence. In 1443, the Jiphyeonjeon became the regents of the crown prince, and in so doing attained an important political status. When the crown prince ascended to the throne as King Munjong in 1450, the political influence of the Jiphyeonjeon grew still further. Just six years later, however, it was disbanded after six of its scholars were executed in a bloody purge by King Sejo (r. 1455-1468).

The Jiphyeonjeon was around for just 37 years, but had played a tremendous role in the intellectual and scientific development of the Joseon era. The body published numerous scholarly tracts, including works on Korean history, geography, farming, and Korean traditional medicine. It is perhaps best known, however, for its contributions to the development of the Korean writing system of Hangeul—just what that role was, however, is still subject to much debate.

Gyeongbokgung Palace's Sujeongjeon Hall. Reconstructed in the 19th century, it was the site where the Jiphyeonjeon congregated to study.

character use in Korean. Proponents of this theory claim that Sejong pushed the project in secret to avoid resistance from conservative Confucian scholars and to strengthen the power of the throne by using the new script to translate the Confucian classics, eliminating the need for a Confucian nobility to run national affairs.

The problem with this theory, however, is that the young scholars who made up the Jiphyeonjeon were largely pro-Sejong. They would play a major role in a number of important projects related to the writing system, including the compilation of the explanatory text *Hunminjeongeum Haerye*. It is unlikely that they would have been shut out of the project of creating and formulating the writing system.

We need scientific and rational evidence in order to conclusively prove who, exactly, invented the Hangeul script. As of now, the best thing to do would be to base one's arguments on the *The Annals of the Joseon Dynasty*. The appeals of scholars who opposed the new alphabet, such as Jeong In-ji and Choe Man-ri, are also valid evidence in revealing who the true creator of Hangeul was.

The most "reasonable" theory, when all is looked at, seems to be that Sejong, the royal family and the scholars of the Jiphyeonjeon all worked together to create the writing system.

## WHY WAS IT INVENTED?

So what was the primary motivation behind the king's creation of Hunminjeongeum?

In the 15th century, the new royal dynasty, now moving on to its fourth king, was in need of legitimacy and public support. King Sejong viewed Hangeul as an important part of his national management strategy. In the tenth year of his reign, there was a rather notorious murder in which a provincial commoner named Kim Hwa killed his own father. This was quite shocking, especially to the deeply Confucian King Sejong, who believed his kingdom should be based on the Confucian belief that the family is the base of the nation. One of the most important tasks of the early Joseon era, in fact, was to figure out how to establish Confucian ethics in community life and beautify social customs.

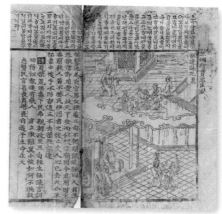

The *Samganghaengsildo*, published in 1481. The book, originally written in Chinese characters, was translated into Hangeul and illustrated so that the unlettered could understand.

Sejong showed immense interest in educating the common people, believing that by educating the masses he could build a healthy society. He believed that the nation would only thrive if he ruled the masses through virtue; if foolish commoners committed mistakes, it was because they didn't know how wrong their actions were. In order to prevent a repeat of the patricide, he had printed in 1434 a book with easy-to-understand illustrations of virtuous models of behavior. While the masses remained illiterate, however, it was possible to educate them only so far. This provided the main impetus for the creation of an easy-to-learn alphabet for the common people.

Moreover, at the time when King Sejong invented Hunminjeongeum, the Ming Dynasty had just come to power in China, which caused the standard pronunciation of Chinese characters to shift from a southern style to a northern style. With the establishment of a new standard pronunciation of Chinese characters, there was a need to adjust and conform the Korean pronunciations of Chinese characters that differed from the new Chinese standard. Since Chinese was the common written language of East Asia, as was the case of Latin in Europe, it was necessary for Koreans to learn the new standard pronunciation. Consequently, there was a need for a writing system that could be used to conform and express the Korean pronunciation of Chinese characters. This was also a key factor in the invention of Hunminjeongeum, which reflects the prevailing circumstances of that time.

*Hunminjeongeum* is a compound word linking *hunmin* and *jeongeum*, which mean "to teach the people" and "proper sounds," respectively. The term *hunmin* takes on a different meaning depending on the relevant perspective. From the point of view of the king and the elite class, it would mean "to teach the people," whereas from the perspective of the common people it means "the people learn" or "the people use."

Thus, the purpose behind the invention of Hangeul can differ somewhat depending on whose point of view is considered. From the perspective of the people, it would be "the sounds that people from all regions may know are the proper sounds," as is stated in an early Ming Dynasty record. Thus, *hunminjeongeum* means both "proper sounds of the letters used by the people" and "proper sounds of the letters used to write our language." Above all, Sejong created Hangeul to make it easier for all of his people to learn to read and write. Of note is the fact that since the Hangeul writing system is a universal writing system that can express not only the sounds of Chinese characters but also the sounds of all world languages, it is more practical and inclusive than any other writing system.

In an age dominated by a Sino-centric world view, the idea that it was only proper for Koreans to abandon the use of classical Chinese, the common written language of the East Asian sphere of civilization at the time, and create a new writing system for the Korean language went against popular opinion. In a way, it was similar to the spirit of reformation shown by the religious reformer and theologian Martin Luther (1483-1546), who was the first to translate the Bible into German and thus contribute to the unification of the German language. As the most distinguished linguist of his time, Sejong recognized that the theory of Chinese phonetics was fundamentally limited in its ability to objectively express the sounds of Chinese characters. The best way to solve this problem was to take the sounds of Chinese characters, which were conventionally divided into syllables, and invent a writing system that divided them into phonemes. And this phonemic writing system had to be both easy to learn and easy to remember.

Reenactment of King Sejong's proclamation of the Hunminjeongeum at Gyeongbokgung Palace

Chapter Four

# KING SEJONG THE GREAT

In the case of King Sejong, the fourth king of the Joseon era, the appellation "The Great" is no self-indulgent exaggeration. Ruling from 1418 to 1450, Sejong was the epitome of the Confucian scholar-king, overseeing a cultural golden age of learning and social development. One of the most enlightened men of his age, he had interests extending far beyond politics and into the realms of science, culture and linguistics. His greatest achievement—and the most relevant to this book—was the creation of the Hangeul writing system.

Sejong was born in 1397, the third son of King Taejong, Joseon's energetic—if perhaps Machiavellian—third monarch. Ordinarily, the presence of two older brothers would have precluded the studious Sejong from ascending to the throne. Fortunately for him, however, his brothers recognized both his skills and their lack thereof. Both intentionally got themselves banished from the royal court—one became a wandering traveler, the other a Buddhist monk—opening the way for Sejong to ascend to the throne in August 1418, at the age of 20.

## National Defense

Sejong wasted no time in utilizing his powers as king. In 1419, the second year of his reign, he launched an expedition against Japanese pirates on the island of Tsushima, quickly conquering the island and bringing the pirates to heel. He also established a series of forts and border stations along Korea's northern frontier to protect Koreans against marauding Chinese and Manchurian nomads. In so doing, he established roughly what is today Korea's northern border with China. In addition, he supported developments in Korean military technology, particularly with the use of gunpowder and cannons.

The Statue of King Sejong at Gwanghwamun Plaza

# CHRONOLOGY OF KING SEJONG THE GREAT

## 1420

1420     King Sejong assembles the Jiphyeonjeon

1429     Jiphyeonjeon publishes the farmers' almanac *Nongsajikseol*

1433     Korean court scholars begin astrological surveys

1434     King Sejong commissions production of maps of Korea

1442     Brilliant scientist Jang Yeong-sil invents world's first rain gauge

## 1397

1397     Sejong is born as the third son of King Taejong

1408     Becomes Grand Prince Chungnyeong

1418     Sejong named crown prince. In the same year, King Taejong abdicates, and Sejong ascends to the throne.

1419     King Sejong launches expedition to destroy pirate bases on Tsushima Island

# 1443

1443　Military expedition against the Manchu launched

1443　Creation of Hangeul completed

1443-5　Medical encyclopedia compiled

1445　His health deteriorating, King Sejong turns over day-to-day administration to the Crown Prince.

1445　*Yongbieocheonga* ("Songs of the Dragons Flying to Heaven") published

© Gyujanggak

# 1450

1446　Promulgation of the *Hunminjeongeum* ("The Proper Sounds for the Instruction of thePeople")

Painting of the proclamation

1447　*Seokbosangjeol* ("Episodes from the Life of Buddha"), *Worincheongangjigok* ("Songs of the Moon Shining on a Thousand Rivers") and *Donggukjeongun* ("The Correct Rhymes of the Eastern Country") published

1450　King Sejong dies at age 53

## Science and Technology

It was in the field of science and technology, in fact, that Sejong would leave some of his most lasting contributions. Sejong's reign represented an age of scientific exploration and discovery. Recognizing talent when he saw it, he became a patron of Jang Yeong-sil, who rose from the bottom of Joseon Korea's social ladder to become one of the leading scientists and inventors in Korean history. With the king's support, Jang made a number of notable advances in Korean science and technology, inventing brilliant new designs for water clocks, armillary spheres, sundials, and, perhaps most importantly, the world's first rain gauge.

Sejong sought to use science and technology to better the lives of his subjects. He commissioned the writing of the *Nongsajikseol* ("Straight Talk on Farming"), a farmers' handbook that contained

Left: Armillary sphere, a model of the celestial sphere, designed by scientist Jang Yeong-sil in 1433

the latest scientific farming methods gathered throughout the country. He also reformed the Korean calendar—then based on the latitude of the Chinese capital of Beijing—to more accurately reflect Korean conditions, and oversaw the writing of treatises on Korean traditional medicine.

## Culture

Sejong took an active interest in the cultural development of his nation. His most important contribution in this regard was the development of the Korean alphabet, Hangeul, but he did more than this. At Gyeongbokgung Palace, he established the Jiphyeonjeon (see p34), a panel of Korea's greatest scholars as selected by Sejong himself. This Joseon-era think tank participated in a variety of scholarly projects: it was this group, in fact, that may

Center: The *Angbuilgu*, a sundial crafted during the reign of King Sejong the Great
Right: The *Jagyeongnu*, a water clock invented by Jang Yeong-sil in 1434

have been responsible for the first formulation of the Hangeul writing system. Sejong also personally composed a number of literary and scholarly tracts, and even took an interest in music, overseeing the development of musical notation, the improvement of musical instrument designs and the composition of orchestral music.

## Social Justice

Sejong sought to lighten the tax burden on the peasant population, whom he regarded as the foundation of the nation. Said the king, "The common people are the foundation of any country. It is only when this foundation is strong that a country may be stable and prosperous." He established a flexible tax code that would reduce taxes on farmers in hard times. He also used grain surpluses to support the destitute.

Prince Sejong reading books

## Sejong the Linguist

While Sejong left behind a great many accomplishments, less well known is the fact that he was a great linguist. From the time of his youth, he had an uncommon interest in academics. There is even a record of his father forbidding him to read and taking away his books because he had grown unhealthy from reading all day and night. One can guess that he was already fairly well established in learning by the time he was a prince.

After becoming king, Sejong

showed a deep knowledge of linguistics. According to the archives of his reign, Sejong boldly rejected a letter of opposition to Hangeul penned by scholar Choe Man-ri (see p54), who claimed that translating the sounds of Chinese characters into Hangeul was absurd. Sejong asked whether Choe understood phonetics, and whether he knew how many tones and letters classical Chinese had. He noted the logical flaws in Choe's linguistic value system, while precisely pointing out the limits to the Idu system. This reflected Sejong's research into Idu and his broad knowledge of linguistics.

Immediately after the creation of Hangeul, Sejong ordered the composition of the *Donggukjeongun* ("The Correct Rhymes of the Eastern Country"), Korea's first pronunciation dictionary, published in the king's name by scholars Sin Suk-ju, Choe Hang, and Park Paeng-nyeon in 1448. This required the transliteration of a good deal of Chinese pronunciations into Hangeul. Yet according to a

*Donggukjeongun*

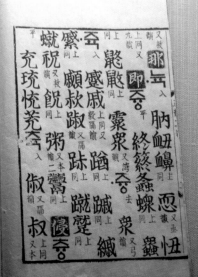

foreword written by Sin Suk-ju, the scholars received approval for each and every word from Sejong himself. Accordingly, one could surmise that the greatest phonology scholar of the age was none other than Sejong himself.

## Legacy

Sejong died in 1450 at the age of 53; he had reigned for about 32 years. Unfortunately, the stability and enlightenment that characterized his reign did not entirely extend beyond his death. His first son, Munjong, died just two years after he took the throne. He was followed by Sejong's young grandson Danjong, who ascended to the throne at the age of 12. After three years on the throne, he was overthrown by Sejong's second son, Sejo, who—while he would prove himself an exceptionally capable king—abolished the Jiphyeonjeon and executed six of its scholars for sedition.

Still, Sejong's many cultural and scientific achievements continued to live on, most notably the Hangeul writing system, which is used by all Korean speakers to this day.

King Sejong the Great's tomb in Yeoju, Gyeonggi Province

## HANGEUL MUSEUM: THE STORY OF KING SEJONG

On October 9, 2009, The Story of King Sejong exhibit opened up in Seoul's Gwanghwamun Plaza. It is a cutting-edge display that teaches visitors about King Sejong the Great's democratic ideals and the creation of Hangeul. Besides Hangeul, the exhibit also displays the variety of scientific tools the king invented. A special exhibit, the Cia-Cia Hangeul Story Hall, explains the Cia-Cia's adoption of Hangeul as an official alphabet and features photographs of local islanders learning the Hangeul script since its adoption.

Foreign visitors can make full use of the exhibit with an audio information system that provides information in English, Japanese, Chinese and Spanish.

• **Hours** 10:30 am to 10:30 pm. Closed Mondays  • **Getting There** Gwanghwamun Station, Line 5, Exit 2. Look for the statue of King Sejong.
• **Tel** (02) 399-1114~6

Chapter Five

# SPREAD OF HANGEUL

**A**t first, Hangeul did not prove particularly popular amongst Korea's learned—and male—elite. The invention of the new writing system was not universally welcomed by Korea's Confucian elite. For some, the objection was ideological: in 1444, the Confucian scholar and official Choe Man-ri denounced the creation of a new script, calling it a shameful departure from Chinese civilizational standards and a mimicking of the ways of the barbarians (see p54). It is believed, however, that some of the elite opposition to Hangeul might have been due to fears of its social impact. Korea's elite enjoyed their positions and power due to their monopoly on literacy and learning; Hangeul—created to improve the lives of the common people—might have been a threat to break that monopoly. Some later kings—Yeonsangun in particular—even banned Hangeul's study and use. Even later, as the Hangeul script grew popular in everyday use, the government avoided its use in official documents until the Daehan Empire period of the late 19th and early 20th centuries.

# PROMOTING LITERACY & WOMEN'S CULTURE

Hangeul had a limited effect on "mainstream" Korean society in the Joseon era—for the political and cultural reasons illustrated above, it was largely ignored by the elite class. Where it did have an impact, however, was in female society (and women's literature), amongst commoners, and in the literary genre of novel writing.

The women of elite households took to the new alphabet, and this would have a profound effect on women's poetry and prose. Through Hangeul, which was invented based on the idea that all subjects—including women—should know how to read and write, the literary life of womenfolk experienced many changes. Women, who were often not given the kind of education that would allow them to use Chinese characters with ease, were able to enjoy a much freer written culture with Hangeul. In the royal court, male retainers would send reports in Hangeul to the queen, who would respond in kind in Hangeul; accordingly, the alphabet became an important means of communication. More and more, women exchanged letters in Hangeul. Even men used Hangeul to write letters to their married daughters or family far

*Hanjungnok* ("A Record of Sorrowful Days"), written in Hangeul by Queen Heongyeong (1735-1815), is a noteworthy example of palace literature. The *Hanjungnok* is also called the *Euphyeollok*, which means "Records of Tears of Blood."

away. A growing number of books, too, were published in Hangeul for women readers, playing a major role in spreading and maintaining the writing system.

The effect the Hangeul writing system had on the lower classes was truly profound. By breaking the stranglehold the elite class held over learning and knowledge, the alphabet radically changed the nature of later Joseon society. For instance, peasants—previously kept ignorant—could now read farmers' almanacs and adjust their farming methods to the seasons. They could read books on medicine; indeed, each household usually had at least someone trained in the basic medical arts. Few societies of its age could boast of such an educated peasantry. It was largely due to the ability to accumulate and hand down knowledge in written form—thanks to the easy-to-learn writing system— that Korea's predominantly rural society could, in the 20th century, make the unprecedentedly rapid transformation into an industrial and digital society with a vibrant knowledge economy. The spread of Hangeul also made possible the adoption of universal education, boosting the knowledge level of the nation and allowing the political system of democracy to take root.

## Novel Writing

One of the more interesting effects of the creation of the Hangeul writing system was that it spurred the development of the novel as a genre of literature. This is not to say that there were no novels in Korea prior to Hangeul. There were, but most were mythological tales written in classical Chinese or mimicking the literary style of Chinese novels. After the creation of Hangeul, however, Korean novel writing really began to take off. The writing of novels in Hangeul, in turn, promoted the spread of the new writing system, so much so that by the 19th century there existed a large class of Koreans who could read and understand Hangeul, from high-ranking state officials to women and even servants and slaves.

## Enforcing Confucian Virtue

Despite its role in freeing the peasants, lower classes and women from illiteracy, the new alphabet conversely strengthened the position of the Korean monarchy. The first work written in Hangeul was the *Yongbieocheonga* ("Songs of the Dragons Flying to Heaven"), a collection of songs that extolled the foundation of the Joseon kingdom and the Joseon royal lineage. This was, in essence, a form of national promotion, now readily digestible by the masses thanks to the new, easy-to-learn alphabet.

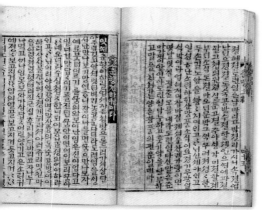

The common people came to enjoy reading Hangeul novels such as *The Story of Chunhyang*, a love story about a young man from an aristocratic family and the daughter of a *gisaeng* (female entertainer) during the Joseon period.

In an effort to propagate the new writing system, King Sejong published a number of books, starting in 1447 with *Yongbieocheonga* ("Songs of the Dragons Flying to Heaven"), the first book published in Hangeul, which praised the achievements of the Joseon Dynasty and his illustrious ancestors.
© Gyujanggak

Hangeul also served to proselytize and enforce Confucian virtue. In 1434, King Sejong commissioned the publication of the *Samganghaengsildo* ("Illustrations of the Virtues of the Three Bonds"), an illustrated guide to Confucian norms. As the text was in Chinese characters, however, it was of limited effectiveness outside the literate elite. In 1481, it was translated into Hangeul, making it one of the first works published in the new writing system.

## KING SEJONG VS. CHOE MAN-RI

Not everyone was happy with the creation of the Hangeul alphabet. The most noted of Hangeul's opponents was Choe Man-ri, the deputy minister for education. In 1444. the scholar-official, along with other Confucian scholars, submitted a written appeal to Sejong stating his opposition to Hangeul. Choe Man-ri's appeal contains his objections to King Sejong the Great's creation of the Hangeul writing system. Seen from a modern perspective, much of the basis of Choi's argument might be hard to accept, but his objections are taken as reflecting the opinion of much of Korea's intellectual elite at the time.

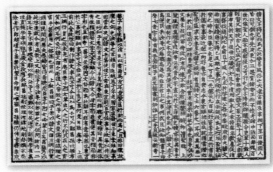

Petition of
Choe Man-ri

## HOW DID HANGEUL STANDARDIZE CHINESE PRONUNCIATION?

Another major effect the new writing system had was to standardize the Korean pronunciation of Chinese characters. One of the first books printed using Hangeul was the *Donggukjeongun* ("The Correct Rhymes of the Eastern Country"), published in 1448. The *Donggukjeongun* sought to unify pronunciations of Chinese characters, about which there was a great deal of confusion in Korea—in 1368, the Ming Dynasty came to power in China, bringing with it a shift from southern Chinese pronunciations to northern Chinese ones. Using the pronunciations of the Chinese Song and Ming Dynasties as reference, the dictionary used Hangeul characters to express the "proper" pronunciation of Chinese characters. Given that Chinese borrowings constitute some 60% of the Korean lexicon, the standardization of pronunciations was a major development.

## HANGEUL IN MODERN TIMES

The Hangeul writing system was finally brought into official use in 1894 as part of a larger modernization scheme and in an effort to promote Korean independence from Chinese influence. Korean elementary schools began using Hangeul texts in 1895, and in 1896 the *Dongnip Sinmun* newspaper was

The first Hangeul newspaper, published in 1896, played a major role in the development of late 19th century Korean society and the enlightenment of the masses. Now part of the National Museum of Korea collection.

established, printed in both Hangeul and English.

Japanese colonial rule in Korea had a profound influence on the development and spread of the Hangeul writing system. With foreign influence in Korea growing in the late 19th century and early 20th century, the class structure of the Joseon era—a major impediment to the spread of Hangeul—collapsed: the so-called Gabo Reform of 1894 saw the legal abolishment of Korea's class system. The Gabo Reform also did away with the once all-

## KOREAN LANGUAGE SOCIETY & JU SI-GYEONG

Playing a major role in the development and promotion of the Hangeul alphabet is the Korean Language Society, founded in 1908 by the pioneering Korean linguist Ju Si-gyeong (1876-1914) as the National Language Research Society. For over a century, the society has worked tirelessly to protect, standardize and spread the writing system, especially during the difficult years of the Japanese colonial era. It was the Korean Language Society, in fact, that coined the term we currently use for the alphabet—Hangeul—in the early 1910s.

Born in Hwanghae Province in what is now North Korea in 1876, Ju moved to Seoul in 1887 and was intrigued by the new Western learning that was just entering Korea at the time. After studying linguistics at some of the new Western-style schools, he found work in 1896 with the *Dongnip Sinmun (The Independent)*, Korea's first Hangeul-only newspaper, founded by independence activist Seo Jae-pil. Realizing the need to standardize the alphabet, he formed with his colleagues the Korean Language System Society in 1886. In 1897, Seo was sent into exile to the United States, and Ju left *The Independent* to write for another newspaper and serve as a Korean instructor for the American missionary W. B. Scranton, the founder of today's Ewha Womans University.

Ju continued to study even while working as an instructor at several different schools; he also ran a Korean language class on Sunday to teach

important Confucian civil service exam, or *gwageo*: the exam, based on China's imperial civil service exam, tested one's knowledge of the Chinese classics and served to reinforce the position of Chinese characters and classical Chinese in Korean society.

Classical Chinese also proved unsuited to coping with the rapid changes that were transforming Korean society in the early 20th century; Hangeul, on the other hand, suited modernization perfectly thanks to its flexibility, ease of use, and wide readership base.

Statue of Ju Si-gyeong

and promote the Hangeul alphabet. In 1908, with Japan's seizure of the Korean Peninsula impending, he founded the National Language Research Society to study and protect the Korean language and its writing system. In a series of works published straight up to his death, he theoretically systematized the Korean language and the Hangeul alphabet.

Just as importantly, his schools produced a number of prominent Korean language scholars. In 1921, several of his former students formed the the Chosun Language Research Society. In 1933, the society published a unified Hangeul orthography, which today serves as the basis for the standard orthography of both North and South Korea.

In 1949, the society adopted the name by which it is currently known, the Korean Language Society. Today it is one of Korea's preeminent bodies on the Korean language, and is responsible for, among other things, assembling dictionaries of the Korean language, publishing academic journals, and conducting the Korean Language Proficiency Test (KLPT) for learners of Korean. Since the Liberation of Korea from colonial rule, it has also promoted the exclusive use of Hangeul (as opposed to the mixed use of Hangeul and Chinese characters) and the use of purely Korean words rather than Chinese loan words.

Classical Chinese also proved unsuited to communicating with and persuading the masses, the overwhelming majority of whom could not read Chinese characters. The *Dongnip Sinmun*, written as it was without Chinese characters, showed itself to be remarkably influential, too.

Reforms in the alphabet were undertaken in 1921 and 1930. The Hangeul writing system itself was standardized in 1912. The Korean Language Research Society (later called the Hangul Society) undertook still further reforms with the release of *Standardized System of Hangul* in 1933. This latter reform became the basis for the modern orthographies of both North and South Korea.

The Hangeul writing system was banned in Korean schools in the later stages of the Japanese colonial era, but Korea's liberation from colonial rule in 1945 was accompanied by a return of the Hangeul alphabet. With the division of the Korean Peninsula into North and South Korea, the separate regimes undertook separate spelling reforms. The last major orthography reform in South Korea was undertaken by the Ministry of Education in 1988.

Today, Hangeul consists of 14 simple consonants, five double letters, one consonant cluster, six simple vowels, four iotized vowels, and one diphthong. Over the centuries, a number of consonants and vowels became obsolete and were dropped. The most frequently encountered of these is ㆍ, the *arae a* ("lower a"), as in 훈글, which can still be found in a number of brand names but has generally fallen into disuse in favor of the "a" ( ㅏ ) sound.

Despite its cold reception and the changes forced upon the alphabet by the vortex of history, Hangeul has now firmly secured its place as the writing system of the Korean people. The alphabet is expected to develop still further, based on its native creativity and scientific excellence, in the digital information society of the future.

The new writing system also boosted Korea's sense of independence and national pride. After all, here was a completely unique system of writing, completely unlike that of China, produced by Koreans for the Korean language. How many languages can make such a boast? Even if this pride might not have been immediately felt by Joseon Korea's Sinocentric elite, many of whom opposed Hangeul as barbaric and dangerously subversive, the writing system would become a symbol of national identity, especially during the dark years of the Japanese colonial era.

## THE MANY NAMES OF HANGEUL

At the time of Hangeul's creation, the *yangban* (aristocrat) literati, who were accustomed to toadyism toward China, did not welcome the arrival of the new writing system, calling it inferior to classical Chinese. For this reason, they referred to texts written in classical Chinese as "true writing" (*jinseo*), while those written in Hangeul were said to be "vulgar writing" (*eonmun*). They also thought of Hangeul as a writing system for women, due to their adherence to a male-dominated society, and referred to it as "woman's writing" (*amkeul*). In addition, it was spurned as "children's writing" (*ahaetgeul*) because it was used by children who could not learn classical Chinese. It was even called "out-writing" (*dwitgeul*), suggesting that it was meant to be read at the outhouse or toilet.

With the advent of the enlightenment period and the launch of Korea's modernization effort, the Korean people rallied around a national spirit and placed a high value on the uniquely Korean writing system of Hangeul, which was referred to as "proper sounds" and "the national script." The individual who created the term "Hangeul" was Ju Si-gyeong (1876-1914), a Korean linguist. What had first been called "Hunminjeongeum," and had been referred to by various names over the years, was thereafter known as Hangeul. In North Korea, it is called Joseongeul ("Korean writing").

6

Chapter Six

# HANGEUL IN THE DIGITAL AGE

Today, Korea is a dynamic country that boasts cutting-edge information technology, an advanced cultural infrastructure, and the ability to produce exceptional forms of culture. At the foundation of this capability is the Hangeul writing system. Sejong's creativity centuries ago, applied as a practical solution to overcome language difficulties, is now revealing its true value in the information-oriented society of the 21st century.

The combination of these vowels and consonants in the initial, medial, and final positions enables the creation of a syllabary. Hangeul's excellence becomes even more evident when the application of modern printing techniques is considered.

Korea's ability to transmit digital content faster than any other country in the world is the result of the Hangeul writing system, which is ideally suited to use with digital technology. Through the Internet, Koreans enjoy an intellectual freedom that enables them to interact with people from around the world and share all manner of information and knowledge. Thanks to today's information-oriented society, Koreans live in a world in which the gap in intellectual standards has been considerably narrowed.

Korea is a world leader in cell phone technology, while the speed with which users can exchange text messages, via cell phone keypads, is unquestionably the fastest in the world. Like Hangeul, Korean cell phone keypads are based on a principle of adding strokes to basic consonants and vowels, which means that a minimal number of keys are needed to create the entire alphabet.

## IDEAL FOR THE INFORMATION SOCIETY

Hangeul is the most efficiently mechanized writing system in East Asia, so it was possible to design Hangeul typewriters that were similar to English typewriters. At first, Hangeul's characteristic method of combining letters to form syllabic blocks made it more difficult to incorporate Hangeul typewriters into everyday life than had been the case with English typewriters. But when computer software in the 20th century became capable of automatically forming Hangeul's syllabic blocks, the inconvenience of mechanical Hangeul typewriters was

The computer keyboard for Korean includes 14 consonant keys on the left and 12 vowel keys on the right. Thanks to this symmetrical arrangement, anyone can easily learn how to create Hangeul documents.

eliminated. That is, a computer can logically calculate whether ㅇ [Ø/ng] following a 가 [ga] should form the syllabic block 강 [gang] or be part of a new syllabic block, as in the case of 가오 [gao]. Such calculations are possible because Hangeul was designed so that syllables beginning with a vowel sound would have a silent ㅇ as a placeholder in the initial position.

Unlike other alphabetic writing systems, Hangeul has a similar number of consonants and vowels. Thus, when designing a keyboard it is possible to arrange consonants and vowels symmetrically, assigning 14 keys to the consonants on the left and 12 keys to the vowels on the right. Because Korean syllables are composed of successions of consonants and vowels, this arrangement allows for a keyboard that is easy to use both

cognitively and ergonomically. Thus, not only is Hangeul easy to learn, but it is also easy to produce Hangeul documents using a computer keyboard without any special training. These advantages hastened the popularization of computers and the Internet in Korea, one factor in the nation's rapid development as a communications technology power.

Cell phone keypads have far fewer keys than computer keyboards, but since there are only eight basic letters in Hangeul before adding strokes or combining letters, sending text messages on a cell phone using Hangeul is more convenient and accessible than is the case with other alphabets. This ease of use and

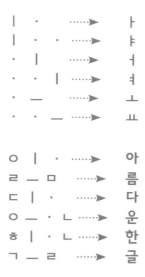

approachability allowed the Korean cell-phone market to expand. Evidence of this is the widespread use of SMS (short messaging service) and derivative products by young Koreans.

Korea's leading cell phone makers applied the basic principles of Hangeul to their text-input methods. One principle that is particularly noteworthy is the "heaven, earth, and humanity" principle. Hangeul is comprised of 14 consonant and 10 vowels, but not all vowels are shown on Korean cell phone keypads. Only the most basic and simplest vowels are shown, and the rest are achieved by adding strokes. When Hangeul was invented in 1443, the concepts of heaven, earth, and humanity were given shape in the three basic vowels of ·, —, and ㅣ. Some cell phone keypads display only these three basic vowels, while others add strokes to these three vowels and display ㅏ (ㅣ + ·), ㅓ (· + ㅣ), ㅗ (· + —), ㅜ

## KOREA WINS SPEED TEXTING WORLD CUP

The Korean team of Bae Yeong-ho and Ha Mok-min won the LG Mobile World Cup, a cell phone speed-texting competition held in New York in January 2010. In the tournament, featuring teams from 13 countries, contestants copied a piece of scrolling text into their handsets—

while the languages differed, the number of characters was the same. This showed that Hangeul, which can express more sounds within the same space, is ideally suited to the mobile environment.

(—+ · ), —, and ] . These efficient keypad input methods, protected by international patents, also act as entry barriers against foreign cell phones.

## HANGEUL AND THE 'DIGITAL NOMAD'

The development of the 21st century information-oriented society is accelerating the creation of more forms of communication, more information, and more original thought. In the process, the demand for efficient linguistic information management technology that goes beyond computer and Internet technology is increasing. Linguistic information management is, in a word, the ability for computers to understand human language, allowing the embodiment of human linguistic knowledge in a computer system so that computers can

Auto navigation systems (GPS) in Korea, like computers and cell phones, also use keypads that efficiently form syllables with additional strokes. © Seo Heon-gang

handle intelligent tasks that once could only be performed by humans. Not only can computers handle tasks such as answering queries like "In what year did King Sejong invent Hangeul?" and automatically summarizing and categorizing documents, but there are already technologies for translating any and every language, which are being improved to be more intelligent.

In this way, it would seem that Hangeul's status in an age of digital civilization that transcends borders and languages and brings the world together as one will continue to improve. Since the time of its invention, Hangeul has made use of the digital theory of "features," so it is well suited to the thoughts and behavior of "digital nomads" who favor mobile equipment. Also, since Hangeul is a phonemic writing system with the characteristics of a syllabic writing system, it may well serve as a bridge between typical alphabets and syllabic writing systems.

Chapter Seven

# GLOBAL HANGEUL

**H**angeul is influencing the linguistic lifestyles of people around the world. A notable task at hand is promoting the use of the Hangeul writing system among those people who have no writing system of their own. In doing so, the extraordinary brilliance of King Sejong's Hangeul can be perpetuated and appreciated by people far beyond the shores of the Korean Peninsula.

## POTENTIAL AS A MULTILINGUAL ALPHABET

Because Hangeul is so rationally structured as a phonemic writing system, and is thus easy to learn, it is suitable for use as a writing system not only in Korean-speaking areas but in other language spheres as well. Just as various language spheres today use Roman script, which has been somewhat adapted to fit their basic languages, Hangeul also has the potential to be used as a writing system for numerous languages. In fact, it is an ideal multilingual writing system in terms of its structure, efficiency, and ease of learning.

For the past several decades, UNESCO 유네스코 has focused its efforts on the elimination of illiteracy by supporting numerous projects around the world designed to improve literacy rates. Despite these measures, UNESCO studies have found that a number of nations still have illiteracy rates of over 50 percent, and that about 20 percent of the world's languages have no established writing system and are thus at extreme risk of disappearing altogether. Especially in the 21st century, when human society has expanded into the cyberspace realm, leading to increasing domination by a handful of globally influential languages, a growing number of non-mainstream languages, which maintain far

Hangeul brush-writing program for foreigners

fewer users, are being steadily shunted aside.

In light of the numerous conflicts and incidents of human strife that are seen the world over, it seems that a future in which everyone can communicate freely and on an equal footing, yet without a loss of cultural and linguistic diversity, might be a pipe dream at best. Nevertheless, all people need to come together to help better our current world situation in which so many people who lack a writing system or are unable to learn writing are being alienated or excluded from the flow of modern civilized society. For those who do not maintain a writing system or lack the opportunity to learn a writing system, Hangeul offers a feasible alternative. In recent years, the tremendous potential of Hangeul as a multilingual writing system has been recognized not only in Korea but abroad as well, with ever more people suggesting that it be adopted as a writing system by people who are struggling to overcome illiteracy.

## KOREAN WRITING SYSTEM GOES GLOBAL

In 2009, UNESCO published *Atlas of the World's Languages in Danger*. According to the survey, of the world's roughly 6,000 languages, about 2,500 are in danger of disappearing. Moreover, over the previous three generations some 200 languages have disappeared, while another 199 are currently on the verge of extinction, with fewer than ten users each.

In the case of the Cia-Cia, a minority tribe of about 60,000 who live on the island of Buton in the Indonesian state of Sulawesi, they have their own language, but not a writing system, so the language faces extinction. With the adoption of Hangeul by the tribe as a formal writing system, however, they can now protect their unique language and leave behind in the form of records the culture and long history of their ancestors, which began flowering long ago with the start of their kingdom.

# THE CIA-CIA

The Cia-Cia language is an Austronesian language spoken by people in and around the town of Bau-Bau on the Indonesian island of Buton. It is closely related to Wolio, the language of a neighboring ethnic group. In the 15th century, immigrants from what is today Malaysia established a kingdom on the island of Buton; in 1540, the king converted to Islam, and the kingdom was transformed into a sultanate that survived until 1960, when the kingdom was integrated into the Republic of Indonesia. Most of the population is engaged in agriculture, fishing, and boat-building.

Traditionally, the Cia-Cia language has been written in a script similar to Jawi, an Arabic-based script traditionally used to write Malay. In 2009, however, the town of Bau-Bau adopted Hangeul as its official writing system with the signing of a memorandum of understanding (MOU) between the Hunminjeongeum Society and Bau-Bau City.

In 2009, the Cia-Cia tribe selected Hangeul as their official writing system.

Cia-Cia language textbook in Hangeul

바하사 찌아찌아 1

이호영 · 황효성 · 아버딘

훈민정음학회

The adoption of Hangeul by the Cia-Cia was due to the fact that no other writing system could better express the unique sounds of the Cia-Cia language. In fact, when Cia-Cia is written down in Hangeul, some 80% of the letters retain their original sounds. Even sounds not found in Hangeul can be expressed using combinations of Hangeul consonants and vowels. It is also said that Hangeul can express the nuances of the Cia-Cia language better than the Roman script. That Hangeul is simple but endlessly flexible, as it was praised by King Sejong in *The Annals of the Joseon Dynasty* when it was first created in 1443, has been proven on a small Indonesian island some 566 years later.

Korea Pavilion
at Shanghai World Expo 2010

# KING SEJONG LITERACY PRIZE

### Recognizing the Fight Against Illiteracy

Upon its founding right after the end of World War II, UNESCO adopted as a prime objective the elimination of world illiteracy. This was because the organization's leadership recognized that the assurance of world peace, development of economies and societies, maintenance of appropriate population levels, and promotion of democracy would not be possible without a decrease in illiteracy.

Since then, UNESCO has diligently undertaken concerted efforts to wipe out illiteracy, which included the establishment in 1989 of the King Sejong Literacy Prize, with funding support from Korea's Ministry of Foreign Affairs. On September 8 of each year, which has been designated International Literacy Day, the UNESCO Headquarters in Paris selects two individuals or groups from developing nations that have contributed to the development and/or diffusion of their mother tongue and awards them a $15,000 prize and the King Sejong Silver Medal.

In 2006, the Mother Child Education Foundation of Turkey and the Youth and Adult Literacy and Education Chair of the Latin American and Caribbean Pedagogical Institute of the Republic of Cuba were so honored by UNESCO. The Mother Child Education Foundation was recognized for contributing to the promotion of women's rights through its "Our Class" distance education program, which has provided instructional content to over 5 million viewers. The Youth and Adult Literacy and Education Chair of the Latin American and Caribbean Pedagogical Institute conducted its "Yes, I Can" program in 15

countries, such as Ecuador, in an effort to advance the potential of individuals and social groups.

In 2007, Tanzania's Children's Book Project and Senegal's Tostan, two nongovernmental organizations, were

Winners of the UNESCO King Sejong Literacy Prize in 2009
©UNESCO / Andrew Wheeler

honored with the prize. The Children's Book Project produces books in Swahili and educates teachers, writers, and publishers, while Tostan works to remedy the plight of women and strengthen the capabilities of regional society.

## Winners of the Sejong Literacy Prize (Recent Laureates)

2009    Nirantar's Khabar Lahariya project (India)
        Tin Tua's Literacy and Non-Formal Education Programme (Burkina Faso)

2008    People's Action Forum, Reflect and HIV/AIDS (Zambia)
        BBC-RAW (Reading and Writing) (UK)

2007    TOSTAN (Senegal)
        The Children's Book Project (United Republic of Tanzania)

2006    Youth and Adult Literacy and Education Chair of the Latin American and Caribbean Pedagogical Institute of the Republic of Cuba (Cuba)
        Mother Child Education Foundation (Turkey)

2005    AULA Cultural Association (Spain)
        GOAL Sudan (Sudan)

2004    Alfabetização Solidária (Brazil)
        The Steering Group of Literacy Education in Qinghai Province (China)

2003    Tembaletu Community Education Centre (South Africa)
        International Reflect Circle (CIRAC) — a network of 350 NGOs and governmental agencies in 60 countries

2002    Regional Centre for Adult Education (based in Egypt)
        Bunyad Literacy Community Council (Pakistan)

2001    Tianshui Education Commission, Gansu Province (China)
        Alfatitbonit/Alfa Desalin Project (Haiti)

# 8

Chapter Eight

# HANGEUL INSPIRES CULTURAL ENDEAVORS

Hangeul is being featured as a unique subject matter in the art world. Items such as designer clothing, cell phones, and neckties are adopting Hangeul as an artistic motif, and this has proven popular with consumers. In this way, Hangeul is more than a means of basic communication, with increasingly diverse applications in the areas of culture and the arts.

Sightings of Hangeul are rapidly increasing abroad, including such examples as Hangeul artwork displayed at the entrance of the UNESCO Headquarters and a Hangeul sculpture displayed at the entrance of the Victoria and Albert Museum in the UK. Hangeul information signs can be seen in the subways of Tokyo, Japan, while Samsung billboards are now a common sight along major roadways in China.

These days, interest in Hangeul is on the rise both inside and outside of Korea. The Korean alphabet has been in the spotlight for a number of reasons, including its scientific and rational structure and graceful beauty.

In the past ten years, Hangeul's reputation has enjoyed a sharp ascent on the global scene as well. Hangeul received much attention when *Hunminjeongeum*, the instructional text providing detailed explanations of how and why Hangeul was invented and the principles of the writing system, was included on UNESCO's Memory of the World Register in October 1997. In line with the elevation of Hangeul's status, it began to be featured as a theme in such areas as fashion, performance, and film. Moreover, in-depth research has been conducted on the distinctive beauty of its letters, ushering in a golden age for Hangeul as a cultural resource.

"Youth," by installation artist Kang Ik-joong. Selected after a strict screening process, the work—based on the Hangeul alphabet—is on permanent display at the UNESCO Headquarters in Paris.

## HANGEUL IN FASHION, DANCE, AND DESIGN

In February 2006, fashion designer Lie Sang Bong presented a line of attire that featured the Hangeul calligraphy of painter Lim Ok-sang in Paris, France. At first, the letters were difficult to make out, but as the model walked down the runway they slowly came alive. The bold black and white brush strokes of Hangeul calligraphy were a perfect complement to the haute couture creations. Lie's inspiration for this fashion line came from a handwritten letter he received from his friend Lim, which impressed him greatly with the stylishness of the Hangeul penmanship. His creations, which have been praised as having "an Asian yet at the same time modern aesthetic" and representing "the harmony

Designer Lee Sang-bong's Hangeul Collection. The dramatic black-and-white brush strokes of Hangeul calligraphy provide an abstract and aesthetic flourish for haute couture creations at a Paris fashion show.

of an abstract formative aesthetic and clothing design," made quite an impression on the fashion world.

As for efforts to bring Hangeul to life, it is necessary to mention the Milmul Modern Dance Company. Founded in 1984, this dance troupe has been performing works that express Hangeul writing through the gracefulness of the human body and dance movement since 1991. This combination of dance, which is known as an "art of the moment," with the letters used to record information is indeed a breath of fresh air. The company continues to develop experimental works, which use the dancers' supple bodies to form Hangeul letters and to symbolize the principles behind the Hangeul writing system as well as its background and history.

## MILMUL MODERN DANCE COMPANY

Founded in 1984, the Milmul Modern Dance Company has contributed much to the development of modern dance in Korea. Led by choreographer and artistic director Lee Sook-jae, the company has come up with a new Hangeul-themed repertoire every year in which the dancers form letters and words with their bodies.

© Milmul Dance Company

## CALLIGRAPHY AND TYPOGRAPHY

The artistic beauty of Hangeul has also been highlighted by the Korean film industry, which is riding a wave of success at home and abroad. It can be seen in the movie posters for such Korean films as *Memories of Murder* (2003), *TaeGukGi: Brotherhood of War* (2003), *The King and the Clown (2005)*, *The Host (2006)*, *Secret Sunshine* (2007), and *Hwangjiny* (2007), all of which feature film titles written in Hangeul calligraphy. Foreign films such as *Transformers* and *Shrek the Third* are no exception, with posters featuring digital penmanship that vividly convey the movie's storyline.

Today, applications of Hangeul for artistic as well as commercial purposes are commonplace and everywhere. For example, at any convenience outlet or mom-and-pop store a plethora of items, including beverages, snacks, and cosmetics, have packaging adorned with a diversity of stylish calligraphy, created with bold brush strokes.

Hangeul is also widely applied to the design of electronic appliances. In October 2006, LG introduced its new Shine Designer's Edition cell phone, which includes on its back side the following verse from the poem "Counting Stars at Night," by the beloved poet Yun Dong-ju, in handwritten lettering: "A reflection of the seasons, the heavens are filled with autumn. With not a single worry, I think I can count all the stars in the autumn sky." This distinctive touch has helped to win over consumers even in the saturated cell phone market.

Designer Lee Geon-maan has been at the forefront of creating consumer products that feature Hangeul and Korea-related motifs. The LG cell phone "Shine." © LG Electronics

Hangeul is also being used as a theme in a variety of other areas, such as ceramics, sculpture, and Western painting, along with Hangeul letter shapes being applied to font design and calligraphy works. There are countless examples of artistic works that reveal Hangeul's natural beauty. And there are ever more instances in which Hangeul is being grafted onto consumer products, often involving brush-stroke Hangeul calligraphy.

At the forefront of the movement to popularize Hangeul calligraphy is the design studio Philmuk, which has produced a variety of works based on brush-stroke Hangeul calligraphy. The studio is actively engaged in a number of fields, such as the production of film posters and book covers, commercials, product logos, signboards, and pattern designs for the surfaces of kimchi refrigerators, which are designed for the proper storage of kimchi.

The graceful forms of Hangeul lettering have led to the development of some 200 Hangeul typefaces, which are used in magazines, newspapers, and books. But outside of publications, there are far fewer choices available. Among the various typefaces,

Some commercial uses of Hangeul

1. Banner celebrating Hangeul on the headquarters of the Ministry of Culture, Sports and Tourism

2. Ceramic representation of Hangeul at The Story of King Sejong at Gwanghwamun Plaza

3. Unique logo design for Green Growth Korea

4. Sign in front of Insa-dong teahouse

5-6. Installation art using Hangeul at Galmi Park

6

Internet content tends to often use either Dodum or Gullim, which are characterized by angular, rigid, and square letters. Bitmap letters are comprised of pixels, leading to a "staircase" effect that gives characters a jagged edge. Dodum and Gullim, which are better than most alternatives, are nonetheless prone to the staircase effect, which contributes to visual fatigue and a lack of aesthetic appeal, due to their irregular letter spacing.

The root cause of these problems is the pervasiveness of the Windows operating system developed by Microsoft, a US software developer, which selects the Hangeul typefaces despite a lack of familiarity with the characteristics of Hangeul. Thus, there is an urgent need for Hangeul fonts to be developed that are easier to read for Internet users. If Hangeul cannot keep pace with this fundamental medium of today's information society, its primary purpose as a means of communication will inevitably be eroded.

Sensing this need, Microsoft is working to provide a better developed Hangeul font environment through easier-to-read, better-quality text, as well as better script support, by adopting a better font technology and addressing existing font issues. As part of this effort, it has linked up with the Hangeul font development firm Sandoll Communication to develop a new User Interface (UI) font, Clear Gothic, for use in monitor display menus and Microsoft programs such as Office and Excel. Through this, users can now enjoy a rich font environment after years of using the Batangche font in Korean Word documents.

One institution that has played a key role in the popularization of Hangeul typefaces is the Chosun Ilbo

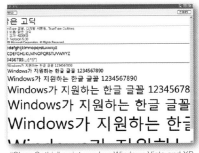

"Clear Gothic" script used on Windows Vista and XP

아름다운 한글  12345678910  abcdefghijklmopqrs
아름다운 한글 12345678910  abcdefghijk
아름다운 한글 1234567 abcdefg
아름다운 한글 1234 abcdef

- Chosun Ilbo Myeongjo Regular

아름다운 한글  12345678910  abcdefghijklmopqrs
아름다운 한글 12345678910  abcdefghijk
아름다운 한글 1234567 abcdefg
아름다운 한글 1234 abcdef

- Seoul Namsanche Bold

아름다운 한글  12345678910  abcdefghijklmopqrs
아름다운 한글 12345678910  abcdefghijk
아름다운 한글 1234567 abcdefg
아름다운 한글 1234 abcdef

- Seoul Hangangche  Medium

"Seoul Script," which references notable Seoul assets such as the Hangang River and Mt. Namsan, was created to boost pride in Korea's unique language.

## TYPOGRAPHIC DESIGNER AHN SANG-SOO

Efforts to design typefaces are closely related to the development of typography. Korea's leading typographic designer is Ahn Sang-soo, who developed a keen interest in Hangeul typography in the early 1980s. As layout designer for the monthly magazine *Madang*, he created the Madang typeface to overcome the general monotony and rigidity of existing Hangeul typefaces. In 1985, he founded the graphics design firm Ahn Graphics and introduced his namesake typeface.

Previously, Hangeul could not escape from its traditional square frame. But the Ahn Sang-soo typeface broke free of this convention, and promoted the diversity of Hangeul typefaces. Ahn has continued to explore new shapes and forms for Hangeul through the introduction of highly creative innovations.

The German city of Leipzig awarded Ahn Sang-soo the 2007 Gutenberg-Preis*, while taking note that "he is a typographer with a rare artistic ability and a distinctive sensibility, and through his innovative typeface development and typographic design he has contributed dramatically to the renovation of Hangeul typography."

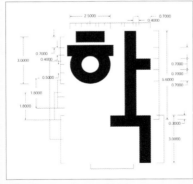

Ahn Sang-soo Font Module

* The Gutenberg-Preis was established in 1959 to commemorate Johannes Gutenberg (1398-1468), the inventor of movable metal type. It is awarded to individuals and organizations that contribute to the development of typography, as well as book illustration, editing, and production.

daily newspaper. The typeface that the newspaper introduced in 2000 was developed after five years of research into a design especially for Internet use. Initiative in the development of typography has usually been undertaken by newspapers, which is true of Korea as well. In early 2007, the Chosun Ilbo made available the Chosun Ilbo Myeongjo Typeface for free, providing newspapers with an opportunity to adopt a Hangeul typeface specifically designed for today's print medium. In addition, the Hankyoreh newspaper and the Samsung Group have also published their own research findings on Hangeul typefaces, which hopefully suggest that related efforts will be implemented in the future.

Cities have joined the media and companies in developing new scripts. Seoul Metropolitan Government announced in August 2008 the creation of seven new fonts to boost the city's identity and brand value, including the Ming-style Seoul Hangangche (Light and Medium) and Gothic-type Seoul Namsanche fonts (Light, Medium, Bold and Extra Bold). The new fonts were developed to reflect Seoul's history, traditions, culture, and society, but with a modern touch. A vertical script was also developed for use on signboards and signs. Seoul—where a scientific writing system was developed with the people in mind and the world's first metal movable type was invented—has succeeded in developing unique fonts that can only be found there and that boosts pride in the Hangeul writing system and express the city's unique identity.

# INSPIRATION FOR CULTURAL PURSUITS

After its invention, Hunminjeongeum did not immediately gain widespread acceptance. The elite class disparagingly referred to it as "vulgar writing," "women's writing," and "children's writing," while during the Japanese colonial period (1910-1945) the use of

Hangeul was prohibited as part of the colonial government's campaign to suppress Korean culture, which forced Hangeul underground. Yet Hangeul managed to survive these difficult times and is now considered an exceptional writing system both at home and abroad, in addition to being actively used to create new artistic and cultural works.

It is gratifying to see how Hangeul can serve as a source of inspiration for cultural endeavors as well as commercial applications. Indeed, Hangeul is no longer limited to the domain of linguists, as people around the world are gradually taking an interest in this one-of-a-kind writing system. Thanks to the Hallyu (Korean Wave) and the growing influence of leading corporate enterprises as they take deeper root in global markets, ever more individuals are coming to Korea to study Korean, while the number of students majoring in Korea-related fields in other countries is rapidly increasing as well. In line with the rise of Hangeul's cultural value, Koreans must further refine the applications of Hangeul so that it can continue to serve as a wellspring of creativity and innovation.

# Various Hangeul Typefaces

뿌리 깊은 나무는 바람에 흔들리지 않으니

탈윤체 Talyunche Font

뿌리 깊은 나무는 바람에 흔들리지 않으니

태백산맥 Taebaeksanmaek Font

뿌리 깊은 나무는 바람에 흔들리지 않으니

율려 Yullyeo Font

뿌리 깊은 나무는 바람에 흔들리지 않으니

안상수 Ahn Sang-soo Font

뿌리 깊은 나무는 바람에 흔들리지 않으니

초코쿠키 Chocolate Cookie Font

뿌리 깊은 나무는 바람에 흔들리지 않으니

쿨재즈 Cool Jazz Font

뿌리 깊은 나무는 바람에 흔들리지 않으니

문화 Munhwa Font

뿌리 깊은 나무는 바람에 흔들리지 않으니

궁서 Gungseo Font

뿌리 깊은 나무는 바람에 흔들리지 않으니

곰팡이  Gompangi Font

뿌리 깊은 나무는 바람에 흔들리지 않으니

맹꽁이  Maengkkongi Font

뿌리 깊은 나무는 바람에 흔들리지 않으니

사오정  Saojeong Font

뿌리 깊은 나무는 바람에 흔들리지 않으니

불탄고딕  Bultan Gothic Font

뿌리 깊은 나무는 바람에 흔들리지 않으니

아스팔트  Asphalt Font

뿌리 깊은 나무는 바람에 흔들리지 않으니

아이리스  Iris Font

뿌리 깊은 나무는 바람에 흔들리지 않으니

우리목각  Uri Mokgak Font

뿌리 깊은 나무는 바람에 흔들리지 않으니

운현궁  Unhyeongung Font

뿌리 깊은 나무는 바람에 흔들리지 않으니

자유  Jayu Font

# APPENDIX

# INFORMATION FOR STUDYING KOREAN

With the ongoing international diffusion of Korean, Hangeul is no longer an alien writing system to the peoples of the world. There are some 20 universities and graduate schools that offer Korean-language majors to foreigners residing in Korea who are interested in learning Korean as a second or foreign language. In addition to these formal educational institutions, there are some 150 educational institutions associated with various universities, including international language institutes and foreign-language centers. This number would increase dramatically if private language institutes were also included.

According to the Korea Foundation's "White Paper on Overseas Korean Studies" (2007), some 735 universities around the world

offered courses in Korean Studies in 2005. According to data compiled by the International Korean Language Foundation (IKLF), in 2005, there were 380 universities in Northeast Asia that provided courses in Korean Studies and some 640 universities with courses in Korean Studies in Europe, the Americas, Africa, Oceania, and other regions.

These numbers are rather insignificant when compared to those for languages that have many more speakers worldwide, such as English or Chinese. But the day is fast approaching when Hangeul will claim its place as a legitimate international writing system that links Korea and the global community—along with bringing the world as a whole closer together—thereby establishing Korean as an international language.

# LANGUAGE SCHOOLS

## KOREAN LANGUAGE SCHOOLS IN KOREA

If you're really serious about learning Korean, you're going to want to enroll in a Korean language school or a specialized Korean language program attached to a university.

### Seoul

- **Chung-Ang Univ. Language Institute**
  **Tel** 02-820-6237        **Website** http://korean.cau.ac.kr
- **Dongguk Univ. Center for Korean Language Education**
  **Tel** 02-2260-3472        **Website** http://iie.dongguk.edu
- **Ewha Language Center**
  **Tel** 02-3277-3183        **Website** http://elc.ewha.ac.kr
- **Hansung Univ. Korean Language Institute**
  **Tel** 02-760-4374        **Website** http://language.hansung.ac.kr

- **Hankuk Univ. of Foreign Studies, Center for Korean Language & Culture**
  **Tel** 02-2173-2260　　**Website** www.hufs.ac.kr/hufskorean
- **Hongik Univ. Korean Language Institute**
  **Tel** 02-320-1368　　**Website** http://huniv.hongik.ac.kr/HILEC
- **Konkuk Univ. Language Institute**
  **Tel** 02-450-3075　　**Website** http://kfli.konkuk.ac.kr
- **KMU Institute of International Education**
  **Tel** 02-910-5815　　**Website** http://iie.kookmin.ac.kr
- **Korea Univ. Korean Language & Culture Center**
  **Tel** 02-3290-2971　　**Website** http://kola.korea.ac.kr
- **Kwangwoon Univ. Institute of Language Education**
  **Tel** 02-940-5304~6　　**Website** http://kile.kw.ac.kr
- **Kyung Hee Univ. Institute of International Education**
  **Tel** 02-961-0081　　**Website** http://kor.iie.ac.kr
- **Myongji Univ. Institute of International Education**
  **Tel** 02-300-1511　　**Website** www.mju.ac.kr
- **Seoul National Univ. Language Education Institute**
  **Tel** 02-880-5483　　**Website** http://language.snu.ac.kr
- **Sogang Univ. Korean Language Education Center**
  **Tel** 02-705-8088~9　　**Website** http://klec.sogang.ac.kr
- **Sookmyung Women's Univ.  International Institute of Language Education**
  **Tel** 02-710-9165　　**Website** www.lingua-express.com
- **SungKongHoe Univ. Korea Language School**
  **Tel** 02- 2610-4802　　**Website** http://studykorean.skhu.ac.kr
- **Sungkyunkwan Univ. Sungkyun Language Institute**
  **Tel** 02-760-1341　　**Website** http://home.skku.edu/~sli
- **Yonsei Univ. Korea Language Institute**
  **Tel** 02-2123-8550~2　　**Website** www.yskli.com

## Incheon-Gyeonggi Area

- **Inchon Univ. Language Institute**
  **Tel** 032-835-9551　　**Website** http://english.incheon.ac.kr
- **INHA Language Training Center**
  **Tel** 032-860-8272　　**Website** http://site.inha.ac.kr/ltc
- **Dankook Univ. International Language School**
  **Tel** 031-8005-2601　　**Website** http://k2.dankook.ac.kr/user/ildku

- Hallym University Korean Language Education Center
  **Tel** 033-248-2973 **Website** www.klec.or.kr
- Hanyang University-Ansan International Language Institute
  **Tel** 031-400-5842 **Website** http://ili.hanyang.ac.kr
- Kimpo College International Education Center
  **Tel** 031-999-4650 **Website** http://kiec.kimpo.ac.kr

## Daejeon-Chungcheong Area

- Chungbook Univ. CBNU International Education Center
  **Tel** 043-261-3214 **Website** http://cie.chungbuk.ac.kr
- Chungnam National Univ. Korea Language Education Center
  **Tel** 042-821-8804 **Website** http://dream.cnu.ac.kr
- Hoseo Univ. Hoseo International Exchange & Education Center
  **Tel** 042-541-5273 **Website** http://ieec.hoseo.edu
- Paichai Univ. Educational Center for Korean as a Foreign Language
  **Tel** 042-520-5730 **Website** http://w2.pcu.ac.kr/~eckfl/renewal
- Sun Moon Univ. Korean Language Institute
  **Tel** 041-559-1333 **Website** http://kli.sunmoon.ac.kr

## Busan

- Dong-A Univ. Office of International Affairs
  **Tel** 051-200-6342 **Website** http://global.donga.ac.kr
- Dongeui Univ. Center of Korean
  **Tel** 051-890-1770 **Website** http://language.deu.ac.kr
- Dongseo Language Center
  **Tel** 051-320-2097 **Website** http://kowon.dongseo.ac.kr
- PNU International Language Institute
  **Tel** 051-510-1984 **Website** http://pnuls.pusan.ac.kr
- Silla Univ. Korean Language Education Center
  **Tel** 051-999-5755 **Website** http://klec.silla.ac.kr

## Gyeongsang Area

- GyeongSang National Univ. School of Language Education
  **Tel** 055-751-6169 **Website** http://english.gsnu.ac.kr
- Kyungpook National Univ. Language Institute
  **Tel** 053-950-6731 **Website** http://lang.knu.ac.kr

- Ulsan Univ. Center of International Affairs and Education
  **Tel** 052-259-2079          **Website** http://int.ulsan.ac.kr

## Private Language Academies

Private language academies, cheaper than university programs, are a good option for working folk who need flexibility in their study hours. Be sure to check out the academy beforehand, however—quality of classes tends to fluctuate from academy to academy.

- Center for International Education (Daegu)
  **Tel** 053-580-6357          **Website** http://intlcenter.kmu.ac.kr
- Easy Korean Academy (Seoul)
  **Tel** 02-511-9314          **Website** www.edukorean.com/English/index/
- Ganada Korean Language Institute (Seoul)
  **Tel** 02-332-6003          **Website** www.ganadakorean.com
- Seoul Korean Academy (Seoul)
  **Tel** 02-563-3226          **Website** http://.seoul-kla.com

## Free Korean Language Courses

Some volunteer groups and civic organizations, especially those dealing with migrant laborers, offer free Korean classes.

- Seoul Global Center
  **Tel** 02-1688-0120          **Website** http://www.global.seoul.go.kr
- Migrant Workers' Welfare Society in Korea
  **Tel** 02-858-4115~8          **Website** www.miwel.or.kr
- Korea Migrants' Center
  **Tel** 02-6900-8000          **Website** www.migrantok.org
- Korea Foundation Volunteer Network
  **Tel** 02-2151-6500          **Website** http://volunteer.kf.or.kr
- With Migrants
  **Tel** 02-3672-9472          **Website** http://withmigrants.org/xe/

## Local District Offices

The district offices of Nowon-gu, Eunpyeong-gu, Yangcheon-gu, Guro-gu, Gangdong-gu, Seongbuk-gu, Yongsan-gu and Jongno-gu in Seoul offer Korean classes for resident foreigners. Days and times differ from district to district.

## Language Exchange

Of course, another option for those wishing to learn Korean is the ever-popular "language exchange," where you teach your language to a Korean in return for him or her teaching you Korean. The personal ads of Korea's English-language newspapers and magazines often have ads for language exchanges. Other places you might check out include:

- Ewha Language Exchange Bulletin Board
  **Website** http://elc.ewha.ac.kr:1004/en/template/sitemap.asp
- Galbijim Wiki Community
  **Website** http://wiki.galbijim.com/Portal:Learning_Korean

## OVERSEAS KOREAN INSTITUTIONS

These institutions provide Korean news and keep collections of Korean educational materials for the benefit of overseas Koreans in various countries around the world.

- Instituto Educativo Coreano Argentino (Argentina)
  **Tel** +54-11-4807-1056          **Website** http://ieka.net
- Korean Education Center (Australia)
  **Tel** +61-2-9261-8033, 8044, 8055          **Website** www.auskolsa.org
- Korean Education Center (Canada)
  **Tel** +1-416-920-3809          **Website** www.cakec.com
- Etudier en Corée (France)
  **Tel** +33-01-4753-6977, 6991          **Website** www.educoree.fr
- Koreanischen Erziehungsinstitut in Deutschland (Germany)
  **Tel** +49-069-9567-5231          **Website** www.keid.de
- Korean Education Center (Paraguay)
  **Tel** +595-21-334-939          **Website** www.kecp.or.kr
- Korean Education Center (Vladivostok)
  **Tel** +7-4232-515-303          **Website** http://kecvl.webvista.kr
- Korean Education Center (New York)
  **Tel** +1-646-674-6051          **Website** www.nykoredu.org
- The Korean Education Institution Network (Japan)
  **Tel** +81-3-6435-1418          **Website** www.kankoku.or.kr

※ You can find more information about Korean studies programs worldwide at www.clickkorea.or.kr/koreanstudies/ks_ins.asp.

# MEDIA LEARNING

## STUDYING KOREAN ON THE INTERNET

- **KOSNET (Korean Language Study on the Internet)** www.kosnet.go.kr
  KOSNET provides on-line services including information on Korean education centers, Korean schools, and Saturday schools (weekend Korean schools).

- **Learn Korean** www.learn-korean.net
  An independent, on-line Korean learning resource site, offering various free learning tools for speaking, reading and writing and a unique on-line forum.

- **KBS World – Let's Learn Korean**
  http://rki.kbs.co.kr/learn_korean/lessons/e_index.htm
  Provides free Korean language study materials in a variety of languages for use by students around the world. Featuring basic conversation, everyday conversation classes, flash dialog, dialog AOD and lesson AOD. Services in English, German, French, Spanish, Arabic, Russian, Indonesian, Chinese and Japanese.

- **Let's Learn Korean with VANK** http://learnkorean.prkorea.com/
  Free Korean language study site run by VANK (Voluntary Agency Network of Korea). With Korean classes, culture, history and more.

- **Cours de Coréen** www.cours-coreen.fr/index.php
  Korean lessons in French

- **Korean Language Education Clearinghouse (KLEC), Monash University**
  http://arts.monash.edu.au/korean/klec
  KLEC aims to provide a wide range of resources and services for Korean language educators and learners, mostly free of charge.

- **Korean Language Education Center, Sogang University**
  http://Korean.sogang.ac.kr
  Sogang University was established with the goal of making Korean culture and the Korean language more widely known throughout the world. Consisting of introductions to Korea and its language, guides to pronouncing letters of the alphabet, three novice stages, and three

intermediate stages, this program has a strong spoken element. It provides flash animation, practice exercises, vocabulary, grammar, reading, and listening. Inquiries can be sent by email to a teacher. Free.

- **LearnKorean.com** www.learnkorean.com

This site was originally designed to help students taking Korean classes. Learnkorean.com provides services that may help your Korean language learning, including Korean for fun, Korean classes, *hanja* (Chinese character) classes, and news from Korea.

- **Life in Korea** www.lifeinkorea.com/language

Life in Korea presents information about Korea for foreigners, specializing in Korean tourism and culture. The site also provides free Korean language classes.

- **Berkeley Language Center** www.language.berkeley.edu

This on-line program aims to help students improve intermediate level Korean through language and culture. Each lesson is composed of a dialogue, a short narrative, vocabulary, grammar notes, and exercises.

- **KoreanClass101** www.koreanclass101.com/

KoreanClass101.com is designed to make learning the Korean language easy and fun, while also incorporating culture and current issues into its lessons.

## LEARNING KOREAN ON TV

- **Let's Speak Korean at Arirang TV** www.arirang.co.kr/Tv/Lets_Whats_On.asp

One of the best ways to overcome culture shock and adjust better to the surroundings of Korea is by learning the language, which helps to reveal the mentality, attitudes, values, characteristics, humor, and culture of the country.

- **EBS Beginner's Korean** http://home.ebs.co.kr/beginning/index.html

Broadcast every Monday to Wednesday, 4:30 pm on EBS PLUS2
Classes conducted in Chinese (Mon), Vietnamese (Tue), and Tagalog (Wed). These programs help foreign migrants such as international spouses and workers adapt more easily to Korean life by teaching basic Korean language skills.

• **Screen Korean**  http://home.ebs.co.kr/screenkorean/index.html
Learn to talk like a real Korean the easy and fun way: through film.
Terrestrial: Thu, Fri 1:40 pm to 2:10 pm
Plus 2: Thu, Fri 3:20 pm to 3:50 pm

## HANGEUL-RELATED WEBSITES

• **Digital Hangeul Museum**  www.hangeulmuseum.org

• **Hangeul Foundation**  www.hangul.or.kr
Introduces the history of Hangeul and the works of King Sejong, along
with the motives and aims of Hunminjeongeum. Explains the consonants
and vowels of Hangeul and contains the official orthographical rules of
the Educational Department.

• **Hangeul Institute**  www.hangeul.or.kr
Contains a collection of Hangeul orthography and standard language.
Also includes the public hearing regarding the enactment of Hangeul Day
as a national holiday. Introduction to the dictionary published by the
institute and resources regarding the study of the national language.

• **Korean Language Institute**  www.koling.org
A collection of master's and doctoral dissertations along with literary
documents from the classical period, Middle Ages, and up to the present.
Introduces its monthly presentation and seasonal Arts and Sciences
contest along with its research activities; also contains an index of each
member's papers.

• **National Language Love**  Café.daum.net/koreantruelove
An online community regarding the national language, lectures about
Korean, information exchange. Contains a participatory discussion board
for foreigners.

• **Korean Language Globalization Foundation**  www.glokorean.org

• **Language Learning Center**  urimal.cs.pusan.ac.kr
Contains words that are commonly misspelled or misused, current
events concerning national language, and the newly changed names of
the administrative districts. Provides Korean orthography, grammatical
rules, and a converter for Romanized Korean pronunciation.

# * TEST OF PROFICIENCY IN KOREAN (TOPIK )

- **Information:** Korean Language & Culture Foundation (www.kolang.or.kr)
- **Categories of Test**
  1. Standard Test of Proficiency in Korean (Standard TOPIK, S-TOPIK)
  - Measuring and evaluating proficiency in Korean required for academic purposes such as understanding Korean culture and studying in Korea
  2. Test of Proficiency for Business in Korean (Business TOPIK, B-TOPIK)
  - Measuring and evaluating communication ability required for everyday life and employment in Korean companies
- **Applicant Qualifications:** Tests are designed for non-native speakers of Korean, including overseas Koreans
- **Administering Organization:** Korean Institute for Curriculum and Evaluation, Ministry of Education, Science and Technology
- **Countries and Regions Conducting Tests:** 13 regions in Korea, plus 114 regions in 35 other countries
- **Examination Period:** Held twice each year at different times according to region. America, Europe, Oceania: First test – April (Saturday), second test – September (Saturday). Asia: April (Sunday), September (Sunday)
- **Application:** On-line at www.topik.or.kr (available in English & Japanese)

# Further Reading

## BOOKS

Hannas, William C. (1997) *Asia's Orthographic Dilemma*. Honolulu: University of Hawai'i Press.

Hong, Jongseon et al. (2008) *Hangeul in the World*. Seoul: Pagijong Press.

Kim, Jeongsu and King, Ross (2006) *The History and Future of Hangeul: Korea's Indigenous Script*. Folkestone: Global oriental.

Kim-Cho Sek Yen (2002) *The Korean Alphabet of 1446: Expositions OPA, the Visible Speech Sounds Translation With Annotation, Future Applicability*. Amherst, NY: Humanity Books; Ch Op an edition.

Kim-Renaud, Y.–K. (ed) 1997 *The Korean Alphabet: Its History and Structure*. Honolulu: University of Hawai'i Press.

Lee, Iksop (2000) *The Korean Language*. (transl. Robert Ramsey). Albany, NY: State University of New York Press.

Sohn, H.–M. (1999) *The Korean Language*. Cambridge: Cambridge University Press.

Song, J. J. (2005) *The Korean Language: Structure, Use and Context*. London: Routledge.

## JOURNAL ARTICLES

Kim, Jongmyung (2007) "King Sejong's Buddhist Faith and the Invention of the Korean Alphabet: A Historical Perspective." *Korea Journal*, Vol. 47 (3), pp134-159.

Silva, David J. (2003) "Western Attitudes Toward the Korean Language: An Overview of Late Nineteenth and Early Twentieth-Century Mission Literature." *Korean Studies*, Vol. 26 (2), pp270–286.

Silva, David J. (2008) "Missionary contributions toward the revaluation of Hangeul in late nineteenth-century Korea." *International Journal of the Sociology of Language*, Vol. 192, pp57–74.

The content of this book has been compiled and edited by Robert Koehler based on the following articles published in *Koreana* Vol. 21, No.3, Autumn 2007.

"The World's Preeminent Writing System: Hangeul" by Lee Sang-gyu.
"Hangeul in the Digital Age" by Ko Chang-soo.
"Hangeul Inspires Cultural Endeavors" by Park Kyung-sik.
"Can Hangeul Help to Bring the World Closer Together?" by Kim Jin-hyeong.

## Contributors

| | |
|---|---|
| **Robert Koehler** | Chief Editor, SEOUL Magazine |
| **Lee Sang-gyu** | Director General, National Institute of the Korean Language |
| **Ko Chang-soo** | Professor, Hansung University, Division of Korean Langauge & Literature |
| **Park Kyung-sik** | Design Reviewer |
| **Kim Jin-hyeong** | Senior Reseacher, The International Korean Language Foundation |

**PHOTOGRAPHS**

| | |
|---|---|
| **Ryu Seung-hoo** | 7, 11, 20, 35, 41, 42, 49, 57, 61, 62, 63, 79, 80, 81, 86 |
| **Yonhap Photo** | 31, 32, 33, 34, 39, 42, 44, 45, 46, 47, 48, 51, 64, 67, 69, 71, 75 |

## Credits

| | |
|---|---|
| Publisher | Kim Hyung-geun |
| | |
| Editor | Lee Jin-hyuk |
| Assisting Editor | Cho Seon-ah |
| Copy Editor | Colin A. Mouat |
| | |
| Designer | Jung Hyun-young |
| Assisting Designer | Lee Bok-hyun |